278

Sharing Stories with friends —
New and old — is a special blessing.
Thank you for giving me that opportunity!
Keep Smiling

A SIMPLE TASK

A simple task to climb a tree —
for children — easy as can be,

With years gone by for you and me —
the simple task is not to be.

Simple, like children climbing a tree,

For work is not what they see,

Reaching upward with
muscles toned —

One step, one branch,
they move along.

Fall they will,
to learn their task

And we must wait below to
catch.

A simple task to climb a tree —

Impossible for you and me,

Downward looks and fear of falling

Will not stop our childrens' calling.

A simple task to climb a tree —

Out of their way so we all can be free.

"*Break the Curse* is packed with purpose and powerful insights. Success will surely follow those who ascribe to the wisdom of *Break the Curse*."

—WALTER PARSHLEY, *Stoughton, MA*

"*Break the Curse* is powerful and insightful; a book you will return to, time and time again. I know I will."

—LINDA OSTRANDER, *Las Cruces, NM*

"Break the Curse is impactful and enlightening: it will make a better person of anyone who reads it."

—DAN JULIANI, *Waltham, MA*

"Steve speaks from the heart in *Break the Curse*. It is truly inspiring and life changing and will teach you how to overcome obstacles in life and business – a must read for all!"

—SERENA FINOCCHIO, *Hull, MA*

"*Break the Curse* establishes "framing" as an essential success skill, making it accessible to all."

—STEVEN RABB, *Sharon, MA*

"*Break the Curse* graciously shares how to overcome obstacles by working harder and smarter. Steve's underlying theme of 'blame no one but yourself' makes this book an important work of international consequence."

—JORGE CARDOSO, *Cambridge, MA*

"Steve Kelley's *Break the Curse* helped me improve my life. His authentic, heartfelt, real-life stories are filled with wisdom, humor, and clear guidance. Whether you are starting out fresh out of school, or restarting a stalled life, the path to success has never been so clearly defined. Pass this wonderful book along to your friends and your children so they can get a head start on their paths. Loved the book!"

—KAREN MCKENNA-VELIOTIS, *Stoughton, MA*

"After reading *Break the Curse*, I realized that nothing stops us from doing what we want but ourselves. Thank you Steve!"

—ANTHONY COSTANZA, *Stoughton, MA*

"*Break the Curse* is a captivating read! Steve gives the reader a front row seat throughout his life journey. He gives you a sense of having lived his life, of having taken part in his victories or defeats, his joy and pain—all while teaching you lessons that will stay with you for a lifetime."

—YOLA ZERA, *Braintree, MA*

"Steve Kelley's unique life experiences form the foundation of this mature and thought-provoking book. It is a mindful exploration of his successes and failures, Kelley shines a bright light on the obstacles and opportunities to live each day in a more conscious, satisfying, and productive way."

—BARRY REED, *Sharon, MA*

STEVE KELLEY

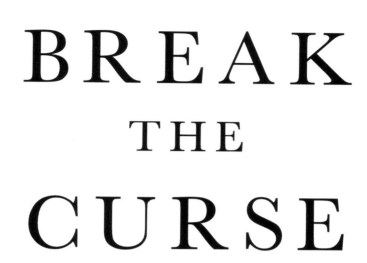

BREAK
THE
CURSE

A TEMPLATE FOR CHANGE

10 Steps to Restart Your Life

One Stop Publishing Group, LLC
www.OneStopPublishing.com

STOUGHTON MASSACHUSETTS

TABLE of CONTENTS

FOREWORD

I have known Steve Kelley since 1993 when he arrived at Cambridge College, committed to finishing his education. When he confided early in the semester about his difficult life and doubts surrounding this decision, I assured him I had taught hundreds of adults who returned to school with the same concerns.

I watched Steve develop this work into a book only he could have penned. It demonstrates his analytical mind, professionalism, and sense of humor, as well as his love of story. Much more than a how-to book, this manuscript draws in the reader through the personal stories of Steve and his friends, whose generously shared expertise and wisdom were acquired through experience. Through these stories, he has made his book powerful and convincing.

Steve says in Step 2 that winners must have two things: definite goals and a burning desire to achieve them. Quite early in his academic career he set a goal to write this book; it remained in his mind and heart for many years. I am so proud that he accomplished his goal. *Break the Curse* is a most enjoyable read because of this sense of determination that shines through. To clarify concepts and theories, Steve laces the text with analogies, sayings, and stories—some familiar, some unique. In life, he says, things happen by chance, choice or crisis, each of which he illustrates with personal examples.

I remember Steve telling me about his house fire and losses which occurred just prior to his entering Cambridge. Several semesters later, my husband Ed and I faced a crisis when, in the middle of the college term, my Ed had to face a triple bypass. Steve, who had taken my husband's storytelling course, came to his rescue by teaching his class and in the process gained experience, confidence, and a part-time faculty appointment. We were so glad to observe his growth and pleased to be called his mentors and friends.

This book addresses not only management but life skills—dealing with conflict, taking care of your body, resisting temptations, building karma, finding your fit, and developing the courage and skills to change. Always underlying the lessons are the values that make one a good person, such as placing family first, continuous improvement, and doing the right thing. This is a practical, entertaining, and insightful book, one to keep, to which you will return time and time again. I know I will!

—Linda Ostrander, D.M.A., Ph.D.
Author, Composer, Professor

DEDICATION

To my grandchildren *Cam, Chloe, Elle,* and *D-3.*

To people like me, who start out with distorted views but eventually
get it right—even with the chips stacked against us.

To those who believed in me and those who didn't;
all inspired me, intentionally or unintentionally.

To *Ed* and *Linda Ostrander,* without whom this
book would never have been written.

To my sister *Mary* who introduced me to my wife, supported me,
and survived with and for me—and I for her.

To my wife, *Susan,* who valiantly pushed and prodded doctors, nurses, staff, and administrators as only a perfect wife and advocate
could do to get me through my stem cell and cancer treatments.

I write for all of you!

ACKNOWLEDGMENTS

In all honesty, the author on the cover of this book is improperly credited. The attribute could easily read, "Authors Steve Kelley and friends." So many wonderful people generously shared great ideas and revisions. Thank you!

If I were to name names—and I am—I offer sincere gratitude to: my mentors, Ed and Linda Ostrander, more than trusted advisors—the bedrock of every good thing in my adult life; my illustrator, Sarah Feragen; my esteemed story researcher, Karen Chace; and my photographers, Derrick Zellman and Lenny Love.

To my editor Carol McAdoo Rehme, whose persistence, patience, and potent methods taught me to share my hard-won life lessons.

Additional thanks to my consultants, Meredith Dunn of Freedom Press, and Pete Kahle of Bloodshot Books, who helped me traverse the publishing world, of which I know so little. Special thanks to my publicist Trina Kaye, our cover artist Charissa Newell, who pours her heart into her work, and to Don Noble for steering me in the right direction.

Thank you to A&A Printing co-owners Bill Ashby Jr. & Bill Ashby Sr. with MaryEllen O'Rourke who streamlined my printing process.

— ACKNOWLEDGMENTS —

Additional thanks to all my proofreaders, especially Erin Hemme Froslie, and to the idea makers:

My wife, Susan, the most natural proofreader ever; my sons David and Phil for holding the fort while I write; my grandchildren Elle, Chloe, Cam, and David III; my stepson Dave and his wife Michelle; my daughter-in-law Jess, who provides so much wiggle room with her twins; my daughter-in-law Rory for her extra-special editing and suggestions; and my wonderful friends Luis, Karen, Jorge, Dan, Ann, Sarah, Wyatt, Alan, Dennis and Rebecca, Rachel, Chris, Owen, Jeff, Roy, Mike, Leo, David, Gina, Kathy, Brad, Dez, Serena, Scott, James, Yola, Sophie, Ray, Mark, Kevin, Rob, Harley, Robert, Bruce, Steven, Len, Ron and Betty, Pat and Jerry, Lynne and Randy, Judy and Earl, Dan and Lorraine, Kevin, David, Dan, Vin, Chris, Shawn, Ramon, Eric, Barry and Cathy, and Luke.

Thanks to the great authors and leaders, Ortega y Gassett, King, Ghandi, Mandela, Maxwell, Eisler, Dana, Ury, Fisher, Drucker, and Bennis whose thinking shaped my life and to others whose work entranced me as they became my best friends, despite never having met me.

Thanks to my website and marketing teams for their great work. And thanks to all of you who support us on social media. Please keep posting and sharing our message of hope, pragmatism, and karma—with great frames!

Thanks to Cambridge College for the opportunity to share and develop ideas with the input of their wonderful customers.

And, of course, I must give my heartfelt appreciation to my Dana-Farber Cancer Institute neuro-oncology and stem-cell transplant teams, doctors, physician assistants, nurse practitioners, nurses, and caregivers who helped me through my cancer journey, including: T. Smith, L. Nayak, A. Torres, B. Virchick, and R. Beaver, and last, but not least, my personal physicians Dr. Andrew Kriegel, and Dr. Yaakov Weinreb (imagine doctors who call you to see how you are doing).

Restarting your life is hard work. It shouldn't be done alone; bring your team to the fight.

INTRODUCTION

I wrote *Break the Curse: A Template for Change* to help people like me recover from the curse of bad leadership and abuse passed down to us through multiple generations.

Like the children of "cursed" families, the COVID-19 pandemic has given everyone a rough start that isn't their fault.

All of us now face a new curse – the COVID-19 Curse. It is a curse that has devastated families, crippled our economies, and tested our faith in God, in government, and ourselves.

Whether you have contracted the virus or not, you are confronted with immense challenges that affect your family, your country, and the world. Break the Curse's ten steps are a template for change to help guide you through those challenges. It is my hope that these ten straightforward steps will help restart the course of your life in a post-COVID-19 world.

MY STORY – Propelled into the future by the tyranny of the past.

I grew up poor on a small, suburban farm in Massachusetts. Our family had five kids. Seven years separated the oldest, my brother, and my youngest sister. My four siblings and I vied for attention from parents who, based on their immature actions, were still children themselves. Everyone in our family had low self-esteem from bad choices and selfish role models. Like many families, alcohol and depression played too strong a part in our parents' (and our) lives. How many generations of bad behavior contributed to our family dynamic is hard to say. But it's safe to say leadership was in short supply for decades in our extended family history.

Our parents were troubled and lost in a myopic world of fighting with each other and battling their own upbringing. Having five children in eight years was not the answer. It was a curse.

Our family income from one breadwinner, a custodian, was very low, and our food for five kids was subsidized. We lived on welfare. A friend of mine said poignantly, "That's not a great place to live."

Back then welfare food, like flour, sugar, and dehydrated milk, came in quart-sized, white bags with three large XXX's printed on the bags. I remember the bags were kept in the front hall closet and we kids weren't allowed in that closet. I was embarrassed by those bags.

My brother was the oldest child. I was a year younger. We had three younger sisters, each a year apart.

One of my more vivid memories was when I was seven years old. I had done something wrong. I don't remember now what I had done.

My mother was screaming at me (again). She grabbed me by a clump of my hair (in anger), and shook me so hard that my hair ripped out of my scalp. I was happy to be free of her grip, and immediately ran away across the street into a small, wooded area. After a few hours, I quietly snuck back into the house and hid in our living room behind the couch until it got dark.

Everyone, including family, friends, and the police, looked for me inside the home and out.

I could hear them screaming my name, but I sat frozen and tightened up in a ball as small as I could behind the couch so no one could see me. I barely breathed whenever I heard someone in the room. I would not come out. Hours turned into a day. They thought I ran away. I was too scared to run away and too scared to be found.

On the second day, my eight-year old brother found me late at night sneaking food in the kitchen and shouted loudly to everyone that he found me. Life isn't fair. He had done the right thing, but we never saw eye-to-eye again.

As this episode showed, very early in my life, I rebelled. I knew our home environment wasn't healthy. From that time on, I escaped from our situation often by stealing away to ride bikes with friends and play sports with reckless abandon. I stayed clear of my parents as much as possible.

I recognized early on that my parents' regular, anger-filled tantrums were not the norm for families. Somehow I stayed positive. I was determined to avoid their mistakes. Instead I made different choices and mistakes of my own. Our family was in a difficult-to-end, destructive cycle.

This destructive cycle was part of the "curse" of having too many children. Calling out having too many children as a "curse" is an uncomfortable frame for many, but it fit our family situation. Each of us kids was headed to a difficult life of unnecessary struggle due to this family "curse."

We all use frames like my family curse to share meaning and convey our beliefs. Frames are important ways we convey our thoughts and our understanding of life. In Step 1, we'll define frames in detail and learn how frames can control outcomes. You cannot underestimate the value and importance of frames, so please pay attention each time we use, and try to capture meaning with, frames when we communicate.

I use the "curse" frame because for my parents, having too many children turned their dreams of a wonderful family upside down. A single child might have fit their parenting abilities, but each child they added to our family added difficulty in an order of magnitude for them and us children.

In contrast to our family dynamic, for some families a larger family fits their parental skills and means. For my parents, more kids was a curse filled with depression and leaderless behavior they passed down to their children.

My parents were trapped in behaviors they had learned from their parents. Passing those behaviors to us kids repeated the cycle causing confusion in us, perpetuating anger for themselves, and unjustified blaming for all of us. As I now know, if I had been born in my parents' shoes, I too might have made their same mistakes and been trapped in this repeating cycle.

Laying blame only fed this disastrous cycle, making it a curse without a cure.

My response or "cure" was to stay away from my parents as much as possible, keeping me at least partly above the negativity. I wasn't close to my parents at all. It was a double-edge sword. The distance allowed me to maintain a more upbeat persona.

As an adult, a friend of mine, after staying with me overnight for a triathlon event, labeled me "nauseatingly bubbly." You might be surprised that I was only slightly offended—because his description fit so well.

He described my attitude perfectly. It was an attitude of resilience that allowed me to create distance from any situation. My attitude gave me space for more awareness, greater understanding, and a small, needed opportunity to think better about life.

Over time I realized that my parents were not good role models, in part because they didn't have good role models. My parents were confused and barely getting by financially and emotionally. My siblings and I followed their bad examples. Life was a whirlwind of incomplete thoughts, selfishness, and poor reasoning. I stayed positive as I tried to break free of the cycle of abuse, negativity, and poor thinking.

Our small farm stabilized us. We cultivated and grew corn, carrots, beets, swiss chard, cucumbers, pumpkins, radishes, green beans, and lots of tomatoes. In the fall, my mother canned what we didn't eat so that the crop wouldn't go to waste, and so we'd have enough food in the winter. To me, with my poor understanding of the world, living in a poor family—gardening, weeding, watering, fertilizing, and turning the fields—seemed like way too much work for little gain. It wasn't fun. I was a child who wanted to get away and play, but farm work consumed too much of our time, overshadowing whatever joyful times we had.

Farm work had replaced my childhood and I didn't like it at all.

All the farm meant to me was WORK, work that I hadn't had the opportunity to buy into before it was decided I would do it.

Still I learned important lessons from farming. We learned the value of hard work as we worked together to survive. We grew healthy produce and even ran a small farm stand on the front lawn. We learned how to appreciate customers with a smile and delivered food to our neighbors for good tips.

Mostly I did what I was told, but deep inside, as evidenced by my run-away episode, I was rebellious. My parents and our family were not in a good place. We were not safe. None of us had a good understanding of our fit in the world. Later in Step 8, we'll re-emphasize how important finding your fit is to restarting your life.

Growing up, for all of us kids, our understanding of life was shackled to the poor behavior of our parents. Their inability to think clearly distorted our views. To help unravel our distorted thinking, let's start by looking deeper into frames and how they control us.

THINK LIKE
A GENIUS

If a person learns and does not think, he will be in a snare.
If he thinks but does not learn, he will be in danger.
~ Confucius

It's never too late to start fresh.

Use Frames When You Think, Talk, and Listen

When you see an aquarium, do you see protected, colorful marine life whose purpose is to amuse you, or do you see entrapped, living sea creatures who belong in their native habitat?

Each viewpoint is valid. Each has a bias. Which is right? Or is neither correct?

Do biased perceptions control our understanding of what we see?

Framing unlocks the answers.

If this is your first exposure to the concept of frames, their ubiquitous power lies just beyond your reach, hidden beneath the surface of your everyday interactions. Like an ocean viewed only from above, you miss the entire ecosystem beneath the surface. You miss the majestic whales, the graceful turtles, the plant life, and the dolphins frolicking in wind-buffeted currents under the water. Equally, these amazing creatures of the sea seem unaware of our existence above them.

In the same way we can't see each other's habitat, the full world hides itself from us because of the biased frames we use.

Understanding framing is the vital first step to improve your life.

For most people, framing is a poorly understood and underutilized key. Prudent action based on clear thinking and clear frames sounds easy, but it isn't.

Think about how many times you've witnessed someone's poor driving, manners, or choices. Like common sense, thinking analytically isn't common at all. A pragmatic thought process requires you to understand the way you frame and how you learned to frame. You need to free yourself from your hidden biases, biases inherent in us all from our upbringings and our environments.

Let me explain by sharing a true story about a bad accident at one of my first jobs in high school.

During high school, I spent my summers installing house and building foundations for a concrete forms company. Jose, the foreman, was a skilled carpenter—and equally skilled at hiding his daytime consumption of wine.

Paul, his right-hand man, was a heroin-using, twenty-two-year-old, inner-city kid who rode shotgun in the cab of the company truck.

Neither my coworkers nor I were on a fast track to a good life. At seventeen, I was the rookie on the crew and sat in the middle of the bench seat between Jose and Paul as we drove to work.

On our way home from a construction site, we got into a dangerous accident caused by a hidden bias we all have, which created a frame we didn't readily see. At an intersection, Jose stopped our heavily loaded, three-ton, flatbed truck and looked over at Paul.

"Let me know when I can go," he said.

Paul looked to his right and responded, "After the red car."

After a car went by, Jose pulled out into the road—and smashed hard into the side of a second car, sending it careening across the street. Our truck was big enough that the crash impact didn't hurt any of us, but the two vehicles blocked the intersection.

Jose and Paul started screaming at each other. I tried to make myself small between them as fists flew violently. Despite my inept defenses, one of them landed a punch on my jaw; another bloodied my lip. None of us bothered to check on the other driver whose car we'd hit.

When the dust settled, Jose was still shouting, "You stupid *#&*#. You told me the road was clear to go!"

Paul pressured back, "You fool. I said to go *after* the *red* car. That first car was *bright orange*, not red. You hit the red car!"

Who was right?

Was the first car *red or bright orange*? I honestly wasn't sure. Did perception cause the accident? If so, how does each of us learn to think that red is red, or that bright orange is really bright orange ...

and not red? I didn't know it at the time, but our concrete crew had just experienced a potent example of the power of frames. In this case, the differing internal frames of Jose and Paul controlled and created the outcome (an accident).

Curiously, unforeseen differences in how color was perceived could have caused our demise. Even the best planning wouldn't have prevented this accident, but understanding frames might have.

The accident and the frames associated with it, stuck with me for life. It's not what we plan for that causes the stumbling blocks in our lives, it's what we miss. We shouldn't miss frames.

Like Jose and Paul, who didn't understand their differences in perception, often we are trapped in our own frames (our internal view) and don't know it. Frames control our lives, even if we don't understand them or realize they exist.

As I wrote Step 1, a news blast came across my phone: Snowstorm causes massive pile-up on Chicago freeway.

What seems like simple, accurate news reporting is not. It shows the bias and frame of the person reporting what he or she sees. If you think clearly, a snowstorm can't cause a traffic pile-up. Bad judgment and tailgating caused the pile-up. Frames truly do affect our views.

Framing isn't just common sense. Framing is more of a sixth sense, an alternate, additional sense that helps you make sense of the world.

That's why I think of framing as a genius tool or skill. In my earlier years, had I been thinking like a genius, I would have acted differently. I would have created better options, vigorously explored different ways others view life, and researched why and how things happen in life.

It took me a long time to realize that frames exist, and that I was using and interpreting information poorly. I was lost and trapped in the small, myopic way I had learned to view the world.

In its simplest form, framing is how we think. Yet it is a complex mental activity, just as walking is a complex physical activity. The complexity of each of these activities is taken for granted. Walking is a practiced capacity learned over time to balance finely tuned motor skills, assess the terrain, and choose and follow a direction. Upon reflection, walking is amazing; our hips move, our knees flex, our ankles swivel; our muscles, ligaments, heart, and blood do their work too. Our brains orchestrate the entire activity, mostly subconsciously. Imagine how hard it is to program a robot to walk.

Programming robots is a skill similar to framing.

Like a paint ball game, as we interact with others, frames are fired at us from all directions. We fire back, too. Bits of the frames we all use splatter on us. Some of the frames stick and blend with our own frames. We brush off frames that don't match our views.

We defend frames that resonate with our core values. Arguments in life are the paint ball games of our intellects. Our positions and the frames we use change as we interact.

Who wins those arguments, i.e., which of the competing frames win?

To find the answer, we need an even better understanding of frames. It is the vital first step to restart your life. Framing is key to clear thinking and powerful actions.

As my own understanding of frames grew, I became more successful. You can, too.

Let's explore further.

Framing is the core of communication. It determines how we convey ideas and how we interpret information conveyed by others. Like a carpenter's tape measure, or a doctor's stethoscope, it is a tool indispensable to the job. Framing also provides the lens through which we interpret information.

When I became aware of frames and uncovered the power of frames, my life improved dramatically. Fast forward with me forty-five years to see more framing at work.

By 2018, at the age of sixty-four, I had worked my whole life to build my real estate and construction businesses with the dream of passing them down to my sons Dave and Phil. But one fateful day, I couldn't find my way home from work, a six-mile route I'd driven thousands of times. I was lost. Confused.

Something was terribly wrong.

It didn't take long for doctors to determine that I had a serious brain tumor in the form of Central Nervous System (CNS) Lymphoma. Only three people in a million get this disease and survival rates are dismal.

My early treatment—including chemotherapy and a stem cell transplant from Dana-Farber Cancer Institute in Boston—saved my life. Had the treatment been unsuccessful, I would have lived only a few months.

Unfortunately, many people experience news like mine. Probably someone you know is dealing with cancer. Immediately after hearing my diagnosis, I pulled my family together for a bowling party to celebrate the next steps we would do together (my course of treatment).

Step 1

You might find a bowling party an odd choice immediately after such news. It was. My family didn't know what to think, but went along without quite understanding my designs. I knew it was important for every member of my team—my family—to have hope. To believe all would be okay, even without a guaranteed outcome. Being positive in the face of the unknown gave us an edge. Of course, even united we didn't have the power to ensure a perfect outcome, but by facing the challenge directly, I felt I wasn't powerless against this insidious cancer.

I was content controlling the only thing I could: my response to the cancer.

I knew it was important to be upfront with everyone in my family. That frame and how I framed this moment in our lives would greatly affect my family. I was at the edge of a cliff with my family holding on to me. I needed them to know that I believed we could land softly.

My frame of positivity steered my family and me to a successful outcome. We did land softly and well. I survived. We also learned an unexpected and recurring truth as we battled my cancer together:

It's not the threats you prepare for that cause your demise, it's what you either don't see or miss entirely.

Asking, "What are we missing?" is as important as any planning you can do.

Understanding Other People's Frames

Once you become aware of other people's frames, you can more quickly and reliably control outcomes. The person who controls the frames usually controls the outcome. Communication through frames is pervasive and potent.

Donald Trump's journey to the presidency in 2016 is perhaps the best modern example of the use and power of frames. Regardless of how you feel about President Trump and/or his policies, he created potent and pervasive frames: "Crooked Hillary." "Low-energy Jeb." "Little Marco." "Lyin' Ted." "CNN, the fake news network." Regardless of whether or not the frames he created and used were true or correct, it is undeniable that those frames were effective in controlling the public's perception and subsequent voting choices.

President Trump created powerful myths through biased frames and correctly gauged how a significant number of voters were getting information from a new, relatively underutilized communication platform, Twitter. His campaign helped disable the media and television news machine, which had controlled the content and access to information, along with the public debate.

By framing the media as purveyors of Fake News, President Trump harnessed the public's disdain for an obviously biased media. He then focused his target audience for his own information campaign and converted the key undecided voters. His approach ushered in a new era of information sharing.

Each time we think, we are framing. Like a painter attempting to capture a horizon of moving clouds and sun, when we convey ideas, we portray what we are seeing at a specific moment. Our interpretation and presentation of what we see (like the artist's brush) expresses our bias, bias that is the product of our past experiences. That bias controls us as we assess, assimilate, and self-direct to make choices in the present. Consequently, the frames we consciously choose, along with the inherent frames from our upbringing, steer us in the choices we make.

Frames are powerful and all encompassing: good/bad, fair/unfair, lucky/unlucky hot/cold, friends/enemies, slow/fast, light/dark, smart/dumb, hard/easy. Even simple, commonly accepted things like tables and chairs are subjective frames, along with concepts like the truck crash into a bright orange, or red, car.

> **To use frames well, we have to be really aware, careful, clever, and circumspect.**

Another good example of a frame is the word *policy*. People and organizations use policy to achieve their agendas. However, we get locked in or confused by this word.

Twenty years ago, I responded to a low-price ad offer at a large retail store: refrigerators-with-free-delivery. I agreed to purchase two refrigerators. However, when I told the Lechmere's salesman the delivery address, he claimed they couldn't give me the free delivery deal.

"The address is more than five miles from our store," he said. "I'm sorry, but that's store policy."

I didn't back down. "*My* policy is to not purchase anything that doesn't have free delivery."

The gentleman called his manager, who promptly changed the store "policy" so the sale could take place. Since the store's priority was increasing sales, my policy was implemented. *Strong frames overtake weak frames.*

Some routinely misapply frames to avoid responsibility and gain personal advantage, often at our expense. Consider a worker who shows up late for work. He tells his boss how his wife got called into work early, so he had to put the kids on the school bus.

"That's why I'm late," he claims.

The worker framed his lateness as a safety concern for his children. While his frame was interesting—"I was being responsible, and therefore I'm late,"—the opposite was true. The worker's frame was self-serving, and lacked authenticity. In actuality, he was irresponsible by showing up late and offered incidental information in an effort to control his boss's view.

His operative frame was: "My wife's job is more important than mine. I can be late. She can't." He clearly avoided any accountability for arranging alternate transportation for his kids.

Even though the worker's skewed excuse may have worked one time, his habit of misapplying and bending frames could cost him his job in the future.

He misapplied the responsibility frame because he didn't think a more truthful admission might be beneficial: he and his wife decided it would be in their family's best interest to use this opportunity for her to get overtime income from her hospital work.

Bottom line, the worker broke his commitment to his boss, but we could also frame this exchange as the boss's inability and/or unwillingness to create sufficient consequences to create compliance with the policies of the business.

To help you see how frames control outcomes and how frames change, let's slow down our theoretical discussion and give you a concrete set of straightforward examples to show how people with different biases and experiences can view and frame the same event.

Consider this scenario: It's winter time and Channel 7 meteorologists just forecast ten to sixteen inches of heavy, wet snow for your metropolitan area. The following are eight different frames for the same event.

Frame ❶

Snowplow driver: Excellent! This sixteen inches should equal about twenty-five hours with overtime. I can pay for that new set of golf clubs.

→ *Internal view: **Snow is a moneymaker.***

Frame ❷

Suburban homeowner: I should have bought that snow blower when it was on sale. My back is sore already. Of course, the wife's car needs snow tires. Maybe I should drive her to work.

→ *Internal view: **Snow complicates my life.***

Frame ❸

Apartment dweller: Sheesh. Bet the city shuts down on-street parking. Public transit probably won't run. Those plow drivers do a crappy job every time it snows. That mayor needs to go!

→ *Internal view: Snow shows government incompetency.*

Frame ❹

Middle school student: Sweet. No school! I'll build an igloo with my friends.

→ *Internal view: Snow is its own reward.*

Frame ❺

Toddler: Yippee! Let's throw snowballs. Let's make a snowman. Let's have hot chocolate with marshmallows!

→ *Internal view: Snow time is playtime.*

Frame ❻

Young mother: Geez, kids in and out all day. Mittens and boots everywhere. Wet stuff to dry. What a mess!

→ *Internal view: Snow is work and trouble.*

Frame **❼**

College student: Fresh powder, dude! Hey, Charlene, let's hit the slopes early. Black diamonds, here we come!

→ *Internal view: Snow means skiing. I'll cut some great lines on the diamond trails to impress my girl.*

Frame **❽**

Photographer: Look at the play of those shadows against such a brilliant white canvas. I'll post these frames on Flickr for sure!

→ *Internal view: Snow is an opportunity to get stunning, sunlit shots.*

So, which frame is correct? Is snow an opportunity? A hassle? A nightmare? An artistic windfall?

All of the frames are correct. Each example provides dimensions or facets of the reality an individual paints when he pulls his bias into his present observation.

As people interact, however, their frames blend, synchronize, sublimate, or in some cases collide with the frames of others.

The results of those interactions ripple outward in unexpected ways with unintended consequences: Arguments and accidents give evidence to how the lack of awareness of frames can negatively impact results.

Let's revisit the red car accident and my foreman Jose's frames with a new awareness of what happens when people's frames (and vehicles) collide.

Jose could have simply stretched forward and looked for oncoming cars himself. Instead, he thought Paul wouldn't advise him to go if it weren't safe. He opted to rely on his coworker's judgment. Obviously, that frame was ineffective.

From this analysis, you can see that multiple frames can come into play depending on a person's *bias, intention, experience,* and *overall understanding.*

This is especially impactful when people experience conflict. Our ability to hold multiple frames or thoughts for the same event is called cognitive dissonance. In Step 5, we'll learn why cognitive dissonance is an important critical skill of conflict management.

Hidden frames carried in words can disempower us. Two particularly good word examples are "student" and "customer." When we think of colleges, we associate quickly with learning, but in doing so we jump right over the business model inherent in the student-college relationship.

Often colleges use that jump to ignore the real business interests of their customers/students.

The business model of colleges is to provide education in exchange for tuition. Within this dynamic, students inordinately subordinate their interests to the provider of said education. Using the *student* frame disempowers the *customer,* who is purchasing an education. Against their own interests, students and their parents unwittingly accept a down-power status, the box prefabricated for them in K-12.

A *customer*, now that's a horse of a different color. We can more effectively reframe the situation if we are aware of the meanings being conveyed. If we, as consumers, position ourselves in keeping with standard business arrangements, we are in fact customers when we attend college. We are paying huge money for a product, money which often creates massive debt that hangs around long after the actual university experience.

As customers, we need to demand that we get huge value for our huge investment in the services provided by colleges. Think how different the results would be from our present reality if college attendees adopted this far-more-appropriate frame.

When we change our view, we are reframing, or repositioning, ourselves or the issue at hand for our own benefit. The more we understand, the more adept we become at reframing issues. Bear in mind:

| ***The person who controls the frames, controls the outcomes.***

Framing is the universal language; frames are ubiquitous. Whether we realize it or not, we speak in frames all the time—which is exhibited in our opinions, both in what we say and in what we leave unsaid. Silence, too, is a frame, and often makes a strong statement.

When we express our opinions, we use frames that reflect our awareness, our assessment of reality, how we assimilate the stimulus we input (past and present), and what direction we want to take. These frames translate and connect us to how we experience the outside world.

Framing is the communication landscape that evidences our bias, intention, perception, and understandings. Framing really is a universal language for human interaction.

As we move forward and understand frames better, let's tie into our theme of restarting your life and see how frames unwittingly affect us.

~~~~~~~~~

Woefully unprepared for college, I predictably flunked my freshman year and took a job with a small house builder. It lasted only a couple of months, but a German coppersmith I met helped me land a job with a roofing company as a laborer. Frank was a great influence on me, since he insisted on safety and perfection—from uniform solder lines in copper valleys, to precise cuts on inside corners of copper gutters, and even to doing thorough clean-up.

As a German immigrant only a generation removed from World War II, Frank faced American biases toward Germans, but I didn't share those biases. Thanks to Frank, I learned the very rudimentary beginnings of the roofing trade. Most importantly, I learned that I didn't like heights!

One day Frank took a day off, and I was sent with a crew to do repairs on a three-story roof in the inner city. The foreman, who scared the hell out of me, stole a radio at the job by opening a second-story window just above the flat roof on which we were working. He told me that if I said anything, he'd beat the crap out of me. I was a scrawny kid, and I believed him. I kept mum.

The following Friday, *I* was fired for stealing. I knew I didn't do it, but I still didn't say anything. So I deserved to be fired, but I didn't see it that way at the time, especially since I got blamed and the real culprit didn't lose his job.

Suddenly, the frames and leaderless habits I had learned in my childhood were exposed.

Step 1

My life spun out of control. I had no job, no money, no skills ... but I had a slight understanding of roofing—dangerous, hard work almost no one wants to do. So at nineteen and not liking heights at all, I started my own roofing business: Solid Roofing Co., Inc.

What could possibly go wrong?

It doesn't take a genius to figure this one out.

Everyone I knew thought I was crazy (this wasn't the last time). My friends were more right than wrong; it was a terrible decision in terms of readiness. One friend proudly ribs me with his memories of my first shingle job, which we did for another friend who was willing to take the risk just to save money (my price was really low).

We spent the first hour on the job reading the installation instructions printed on the bundles of shingles. We actually found a way to do the job so the roof didn't leak and created value for the homeowner as promised. I was firmly on the path of doing things the hard way, but I had embraced change, something that would bode well in my future.

At this point in my life, I should have gone back to college. Without money, I couldn't afford to go. I had few choices. My roofing career was launched with little experience and even less knowledge. Everyone thought I would fail except me: I couldn't think that far ahead. I had no choice but to succeed. Mostly, I was too busy to do more than survive. There was no acceptable fallback position, and I believed in myself. Even if no one else did.

I survived by sheer will alone. I leaned on the old maxim: *Life tests first and teaches afterward.* It kept me on my toes.

Armed with an intense desire to work for what I got, create value in everything I did, and keep my word each time I made a deal, I worked harder and longer than anyone I knew. If it got dark before my helpers and I finished a job, we wore miner lights on our foreheads, something the guys who worked for me grew to hate. I was a hard-ass, hard-pushing, horrible boss, with no HR department for complaints, no sick time for anyone, and few benefits.

It was simple: You work, you get paid. You don't work, you don't get paid. The same rules applied to me. With one big exception. If I bid a job wrong, I worked twice as hard and *didn't* get paid. Regardless of whether or not I got paid, those who worked for me earned an honest living and always received a paycheck. With hard work as a core value, my company did well enough to appear successful. At least to the outside world.

As our work and company grew, I got married, adopted my stepson, Phil, and fathered Dave. Both boys worked hard right alongside me. To this day my kids will tell you that the hair on the back of their necks goes up in dread every time they hear, "Rise and shine, sweethearts! Five minutes!"

On days when the kids didn't have school, at 5:00 a.m. (or earlier), I barked that phrase in a shrill, jarring tone to wake the boys for work.

Back then, daycare amounted to a rope tied to my youngest son's waist, giving just enough slack so he couldn't reach the edge of the roof and fall. And, yes, the boys climbed their way up and down roofs. (For sure, this is not a recommendation for anyone!)

Spending time with my sons was important to me, even though it meant most of our time together was spent on the job. Proudly, I can say it was one of the few great decisions I made in my early career. To this day, continuing with my grandchildren, our family and business core belief is: If we work together and share values, we'll stay together and prosper.

Step 1

We prospered by sheer force of will.

Running a roofing company with little experience and even less wisdom was a long way from anything you could call a strategy or true financial success. Yet thirteen years after establishing my business, we were able to buy an oceanfront, fixer-upper home with a great ocean view. After working our tails off, we moved into our new home and were making our way up the ladder of what we thought was success.

In truth, I was a long way from thinking like a genius, understanding frames, and gaining a better understanding of the world in which I lived. But the seeds for those important steps in my life were planted when we bought our home.

Six years later, on March 13, 1993, our lives tumbled into tumult when an electrical fire burned our house almost completely down.

Fortunately no one was physically hurt in the fire, but I was shaken to my core by the local authorities investigating the fire. After the devastation of the fire, the last thing I expected was to become a suspect in the cause of the fire. But that was exactly what happened.

The investigators were wrong. I hadn't set the fire.

The actual cause was poor installation design of a ground fault interrupter (GFI) on the ocean-facing, exterior kitchen wall. During storms, salty ocean water smashed the sea wall and sprayed against the house, corroding electrical feed wires behind the outlet. The subsequent arcing burned the wood framing in the walls. The GFI had been useless without a GFI breaker to prevent electrical flow.

It was the unhappiest week of my life. Yet something good always comes out of hard lessons.

The day after the fire, fourteen-year-old Dave and I surveyed the damage. Most of the structure was fractured but intact, with axed openings from the fire department's relief efforts and the fire itself. Rear walls were black and burned. Window openings were covered with makeshift plywood. The roof had gaping holes, which exposed the remaining rafters.

The house was a shell of its former self. I felt the same.

As I looked up at the roof, I recalled pictures of London during World War II: hulking, teetering buildings overshadowing the devastation beneath.

Underneath our splintered, charred roof were the water-soaked, ruined remains of our life: soaked and burned clothes, broken tiles, fallen walls, melted wires, crumpled pictures, shattered glass ... and the smell: the acrid, sodden, smoldering wood smell that I couldn't get out of my head for weeks. My home was mutilated, as distorted as my memories were becoming. Like when yesterday becomes fogged out by a more intense today. Only this was permanent.

Dave and I stepped gingerly onto the fire-scorched, soggy carpets of our once-comfortable family room. Everything was saturated, even the plastic stuff. Dirty water dripped down on us from the fire-hose-soaked flooring above. Normally we would have shrugged it off, but now we had no clothes to change into and no place to change into them. Isn't it funny what we worry about when really important things encircle us or, in this case, engulf us?

The stunning ocean view no longer mattered.

Cautiously picking our way up the stairs as far as we could safely go, we eyed Dave's bedroom down the hallway and observed his

Apple IIGS computer (circa 1990), mutilated and melted in a swirling, multi-colored, ice-cream-cone shape over what was left of his desk. Clothes were strewn like shrapnel.

I couldn't connect the dots. My thoughts were curiously discon-nected. *This isn't right. I don't remember his room being that messy. His mother wouldn't like to see this wet rug.*

The scene in front of us was surreal. A beam of sunlight pierced the burned-out roof and lit up Dave's bedroom—and my stoic façade. My ability to hold myself together was being stretched to its limit.

Dave knew I was wrenched by the previous evening's fiery events. But I hadn't told him I was a suspect in the fire. The authorities had made it clear. They thought it was arson.

However, Dave and I were at home together when the fire started. He was the first to observe the smoke coming from the eyeball lights in the kitchen. It completely surprised and shocked us both.

Had he known that I was suspected of setting the fire, he would have realized quickly how impossible it would have been for me to have set the fire without him knowing, never mind the risk that such a despicable act might have brought to his safety and mine. I thanked my lucky stars (if I still had any), that he was with me the night the fire started at the house, and that at least he knew for sure what the truth was.

I was crushed far more by the accusations of wrongdoing than by the devastation of the fire, the insurance company's impending investi-gation, or the prospect of rebuilding. I stared expressionless and deep in thought, grappling with my overarching question: *Why did there have to be a suspect?*

Fires are crazy and unexplainable, aren't they? There is no good reason for a fire, even if there is an actual cause. I had trouble finding an accurate frame.

What was the connection between blame and bad things happening? I blinked back to reality as my son started talking. I had been looking right through him, through the house, and into space.

"Dad ... Dad! Are you with it or what?"

Then, as he gazed thoughtfully at what was left of his belongings, Dave turned his eyes upward toward the sunlight pouring through our roof. With a wry grin, he said, "You know, Dad, I always wanted a skylight!"

With that simple twist of viewpoint, my fourteen-year-old infused me with laughter and hope.

He changed my life with his incredibly mature reframing.

Growing up at age 45

Everything changed after the fire.

The combined stresses of six dedicated months of rebuilding, being a suspect in the fire, fighting with local authorities, and wrestling with insurance issues while simultaneously earning a living were too much. Something had to give, and give it did.

My marriage dissolved.

The ensuing divorce forced me into insolvency. I was busted broke. I was exhausted from the fire, the divorce, the pressure of rebuilding my life. It was a long way back, and the incompleteness of my life was exposed.

We all grow up at different times in our lives, for different reasons and in different ways—sometimes moving forward, or stagnating for a while, or moving back under pressure. Most people grow up sooner than I did. I grew up after the fire.

Growing up meant finally taking responsibility for everything that happened: taking responsibility for the fire, for the divorce, for *every-thing*. It wasn't easy. Like most people in a broken marriage, initially I blamed my mate.

Blaming others does not create success.

After a strongly contested divorce, I was angry at my wife, angry at lawyers and the laws they uphold, angry at authorities who had accused me, angry at myself, angry at the world. I didn't know it, but my anger would instigate an interest in conflict management (which I later would teach at Cambridge College and Curry College in Massachusetts).

With my firsthand experience after the fire and from my studies on conflict, I learned people lose control, embrace anger, and often lose their tempers in very destructive ways when three things cohere. We'll call these The Three Devils:

1. Injury to sense of self (the ego is bruised).

2. Injury to sense of control (the unrelenting desire to always be in a protected, self-driven bubble of control).

3. Injury to sense of rightness to the world (the insidious urge to play the victim role. "That's not fair.").

Each of these devils came calling after the fire. Like an over-filled balloon just released and wildly spinning about, I lost control. My anger was immense. My psyche weakened, I became depressed and lost the balance in my life. Injuries to my ego, control, and sense of rightness created deep, deadly unhappiness.

José Ortega y Gassett, the famous Spanish philosopher, defines unhappiness as "the permanent bruise each and every one of us gets when we come face to face with reality." It's inevitable to be unhappy during difficult times like the fire my family experienced.

We have to bounce back.

Whether unhappiness results from major events like fire, the death of a loved one, divorce, or just smaller disappointments like not being selected for a team, missing a bus, oversleeping, or getting cut off in traffic, conflict hurts and is disruptive. The trick is to think analytically to overcome these abrupt bruises in our day and unseat the perceived and/or actual injuries related to The Three Devils.

Analytical thinking requires us to utilize those frames that most accurately reflect reality while simultaneously creating the best life for ourselves *and* those around us. When Dave reframed our view of devastation to a cheerful pitch for a skylight, I knew he was going to be okay for the rest of his life. I felt better, too. Dave was leading and making the best of the situation by thinking like a genius.

When we think like a genius, we act maturely.

Maturity makes the best of every situation you encounter, not just the easy situations. When people overcome truly difficult circumstances and heroically harness the anger and unhappiness they feel, they act maturely.

In contrast, we suffer when we don't align with reality, regardless of how harsh the reality. Away from reality, we become dependent on false logic. We form bad habits and respond to our challenges immaturely, even childishly.

To be honest, after the fire I did not make the best of my situation. I blamed others for the problems I experienced. By definition, I was immature. As unpredictable and trying as the fire and ensuing consequences were, I needed to make the best of it. Regardless of the stress I felt at the time.

During the aftermath of the fire, my anger fueled a destructive phase. I felt life and The Three Devils were conspiring to knock me down. I fell into a victim role.

Along with painful family issues surrounding the divorce, my net worth was decimated. By the time my ex-wife and I divorced, my net worth had spiraled downward from nearly a million dollars to -$200,000. This amount represented my total debt on the day my divorce was finalized, including the sum of the alimony payments I had yet to make to my ex-wife to satisfy our divorce agreement. In order to pay off the debt, I needed to earn $300,000 so that after taxes I would have the $200,000 to pay the debt.

To this day I chuckle to myself when I hear people talk about being broke. Back then, I could only dream of being broke because I knew I had to earn several hundred thousand dollars just to be able to *call* myself broke.

It was time to grow up. I was late to the party. (Truthfully, it's never too late to grow up, no matter how old you are or what circumstances caused you to be late.) I had to take responsibility for everything that happened: my broken marriage, the overwhelming debt, my own losses, and any hard feelings I had created within the family. All of it. Despite wanting to blame my ex-wife for everything! After all, the easiest thing in the world to do is to blame other people for your problems.

Within the frame of playing the blame game, I couldn't unseat The Three Devils (my ego, my desire to control, and thinking of myself as a victim).

To change and create a better outcome, I had to accept that I was responsible for everything that happened, including what my ex-wife had done, all the vicious gossip and courtroom antics, and everything else.

How could it *all* be my fault, you ask? Because my ex-wife wouldn't have been in my life had I not married her. We didn't have an old-fashioned shotgun wedding. No one *forced* me to marry her.

My recovery started when I learned to own my choices and to adopt a responsibility frame. I began to recognize my responsibility for everything and acknowledge the truth: Things don't just mysteriously happen. I was the primary action agent in my life.

I took ownership for my choices, a watershed moment!

Still, I was missing an essential element before I could move on and press forward. I had to forgive myself. We are all human; we all make mistakes.

Once I forgave myself, I was on a path toward a better life. Except … another pesky problem cropped up. How could I justify forgiving myself yet not forgive the others I had brought into my life? What kind of person would I be if I forgave myself but wouldn't do the same for others? I knew the answer and settled into the difficult task of forgiveness. At last, I could move forward.

A word about forgiveness: When you feel slighted or harmed, forgiving those who are involved isn't an easy task at all, but you'll be shackled to the past if you can't forgive. It is difficult, yet absolutely necessary.

Step 1

The Importance of Place, Past, and Environment

Sociologists routinely make the case that the environment into which we are born shapes both us and our futures. How much of who and what we become can be attributed to the environment we either intentionally place ourselves into or unintentionally accept as our fate? Could it be just the luck of the draw? Are our lives cast in stone by being born into poverty? By being born into wealth?

Is place a controlling factor? A virtual mind and body-snatcher? Or is place more like a rough bobsled ride we stoically endure?

We endure, yet we are controlled to some extent. Our environments imprint us with life-long references built upon our experiences—which subsequently shape and control our actions. We truly are captives to our past.

When I was eight years old, I played barefoot with friends in the schoolyard one steamy summer day. A ten-year-old girl beckoned me to move nearer.

"Over here. Closer," she insisted. "No, not there." She grabbed my shoulders to guide me. "Now, move to the left and look straight ahead."

In search of approval, I willingly complied.

"That's it. You're ... almost ..." she nudged me a bit farther, "there. Now, jump backwards."

Trustfully, I did as she asked—and felt a mushy warmth ooze between my toes. Startled, I looked down.

I had jumped backwards into a pile of pungent dog doo.

Face flushing, I raced away in tears from my gawking, laughing friends. I never spoke to that girl again. I was too embarrassed.

But before you think damning thoughts toward those youngsters, know that I might have pulled the same trick on someone else, had it not happened to me first.

Now, consider a rather unflattering story from my past.

Several years ago while doing a renovation job, I met a technician from the alarm company. He approached me for some work instructions, but couldn't stop staring at me, assessing me with an I-can't-figure-out-where-I-know-you-from look. As I outlined my needs, he appeared to be only half-listening.

"I know you!" he blurted. "You were my basketball coach when I was seven years old."

I didn't recognize this towering 6'6 guy at all. *I hope I was nice to this kid*, I thought. *He could squish me like a bug.*

"I was on your son Dave's team," he prodded. "You coached us."

My mind raced, trying to place him, but I drew a blank.

"Do you remember that game when I got hurt and was benched because I got poked in the eye?"

I shook my head. "No. Not really. It was twenty-five years ago."

"You don't remember what you told me?"

Suddenly a scene flashed through my mind. I could see a skinny kid back in the day. A real nice kid. Karl. His name was Karl. Good kid, good family.

"I'm guessing I said, 'Hang in there kid. Give it a rest, and we'll get you back in the game.'"

His eyes widened before a grin streaked across his face. "Umm, not quite." He paused for effect. "What you said was 'Get back in there or I'll poke your other eye out.'"

Ouch! "Well," I contested his memory, "I'm guessing I didn't say it *that* way."

"Oh, yes," he assured. "You said it that way."

As I think now of my embarrassing coaching and barefoot stories, it's fair to say I wouldn't handle things the same way now. We all do things we are not proud of at different times. We often don't understand the ripple effect of our actions.

> ***Time and understanding are not***
> ***equal in each person's life.***

Often we realize too late that we have harmed someone. We only learn from our experiences when we are ready to learn, and many never learn at all.

In the barefoot episode, I judged my friends too harshly because I believed they should have known the harm their action could cause. We often mistakenly judge people by our own timelines of learning.

We shouldn't.

> *How can we justify pointing out to others the moment they should have learned something? In doing so, we incorrectly present ourselves as a singular time reference to learning life's lessons. We are not the measuring stick and timeline for all learning.*

Yet we all make those judgments as though we are. If we use our personal learning curve as a metric, we judge others myopically and distort reality.

The important frame here, regardless of which side of the encounter you were on, is that past experiences shaped the actions of those involved. The actors in these mini-dramas were simultaneously perpetuating their pre-ordained birthright roles. Each forwarded the behaviors learned in past environments, captives to the past.

As you can see, people are a strong part of place. Unexpected events mold our lives. Each of our lives are shaped by stories just like these.

From these simple stories, it's easy to see why people, place, and environment are so important. Bastardized beginnings and broken homes set the path for far too many of us. Where we come from matters. Overcoming the places we come from matters even more. Yet doing so is extremely difficult.

In early life, if we witness parents, friends, role models, peers, and others acting irresponsibly, with little regard to consequences or societal values that preserve well-being, we too become ensnared in those patterns of behavior. For many, our birthright of place is often a trap with a primary, magnetic pull toward bad behavior.

Even though nobody asks to be born, the uncompromising luck of the draw can be a mean-spirited thing. If you are born into a flawed environment, poor behavior normalizes that poor behavior before you have enough background against which to compare it. Without context, your frames of reference and understanding are slanted and distorted in ways you can't see. As a result, it's nearly impossible to think like a genius, recognize biases, understand frames, and see life clearly.

As humans, we react to our environments with a certain consistency. Generally that behavioral consistency means that if I were born in Person A's shoes, with the influences he/she experienced, and with the IQ and make-up of Person A, then I'd be doing what Person A is doing now, with all the faults or credits that background and environment afford.

Few people across the world are born into the privilege of a good life with good values, especially given the global pressures of poverty, wars, inequality, racial unrest, physical challenges, environmental degradation, catastrophic events, pollution, and the lack of good education.

Instead, most are born into difficult environments, having to work hard to live normal lives. For those of us who come from difficult environments, our upbringing is more of an endurance test than a nurturing experience. Self-preservation and success can only happen when we distance ourselves from our negative primary environment's stranglehold.

I created that distance and change at forty-two, when I went back to school to complete my college degree. It wasn't the education or the degree that made the difference. It was a lucky break that came about when I met Dr. Edmund Ostrander and his wife, Dr. Linda Ostrander. Ed and Linda were teachers and musicians, and Ed was a professional storyteller. When I met Ed and Linda, neither they nor I had any idea how much their influence would help me change my life.

Finding great mentors helped me reverse the magnetic pull of my past. Ed and Linda overlooked the negative behaviors that had stalled my personal growth and recognized the good values I had. Their belief in me gave me an opportunity to excel.

Famed *Blue Zones* author Dan Buettner researched people who live successfully into old age (over 100). Dan states "the longest-lived people in the world live in environments that nudge them into behaviors that foster longevity."

To get to a place that fosters longevity, we need people who can share well-thought-out values. We need people who can help us adopt better values and help us change our behavior.

As my new mentors, Ed and Linda could see that I needed more than a centenarian's "nudge," and they provided more. Together they pulled, pushed, dragged, and molded me into a person I could be proud to be. In the next chapter, you'll learn how Ed, Linda, and I met.

SUMMARY

Frames are pervasive and potent. Frames control outcomes. You must use and analyze frames with great care. Misplaced aggression and anger preclude taking full responsibility for your life. Seek to forgive to uncouple the magnetic pull of your past. Be mindful of the environment you are in and the environment you create with the ripple effects of your actions. As a snake releases its skin, so must we release our past for a better future.

Step 1

Action Steps to Think Like a Genius

1. Start your morning by asking "What is the most effective use of my time today?"

2. Think of your goals as guidance about what is important to you.

3. Prioritize clear thinking. Spend time in reflection, to understand your bias on the issues you confront daily. Think about how you frame your interactions.

4. Carefully analyze the frames others use.

5. Take responsibility for everything in your life.

6. Use email in place of texts and twitter. Text only when texting has real effect for scheduling, etc. Due to the short character allowance and quick-time usage, texts encourage loose and incomplete thinking. The same advice applies to tweets.

7. Write down your thoughts before determining an action. Examine your bias, intention, perception, and understanding. What are you missing?

8. Guard against a victim mentality; it stunts your personal growth.

A genius probably wouldn't...

... *worry about what he/she can't change.*
→ **Genius thinking: leave the past where it belongs.**

... *throw happiness overboard.*
→ **Genius thinking: recognize that you can change and a better life awaits you as you improve your thinking.**

... *spend a lot of time watching television.*
→ **Genius thinking: Well-thought-out ideas are few and far between on TV.**

... *gossip.*
→ **Genius thinking: gossip won't help you become an analytical thinker.**

Our path forward...

~~~~~~

In Step 1, we improved our understanding of frames. We could say we learned to treat our minds as employees and put our minds to work for us.

In Step 2, we'll share the importance of goals and integrate our knowledge of framing with a goal-setting strategy.

SET GOALS

Winners must have two things: definite goals
and the burning desire to achieve them.
~ Brad Burden

Set your goals to let your dreams free

oals provide a powerful influence in our lives. Goals help us achieve what we want by providing direction and focusing our energy. Conversely, without goals, the old maxim applies: "If you don't know where you are going, any road will take you there."

Several years ago, I taught a negotiation class to twenty-five students from all over the world, including six who were from the same country. Those six sat beside each other, continuously whispering back and forth in their native language.

They detracted from their classmates' learning and drove me crazy. Several times I gave them stern looks and asked them to stop talking, to no avail.

Because English was their second language, I didn't know whether they were discussing the lesson or simply not paying attention. I didn't handle it well, and I wasn't happy with them or me.

To get a better result, I reviewed my teaching goal: to create a safe and effective learning environment for all students. That evening I asked myself, "What could I have done to change the outcome?"

When class reconvened the following morning, I made a simple announcement: "Today I'd like you all to sit next to someone from another country. We'll get to know each other better, and learning other cultures is part of being a good negotiator."

Problem solved. No more whispering. The class was far more effective after this significant change.

I had reviewed my goal and changed how I framed my interactions with the students. Everything I said was completely true. No one was the wiser as to how I had reengineered an effective classroom environment. Several of the six students thanked me personally after class for making it an easier place to learn.

By paying close attention, you can see how changing my frame changed the outcome. My original frame was: "This is important stuff I'm teaching. Stop being knuckleheads!" This allowed me to blame the students for their errant behavior.

Digging deeper to understand why the errant behavior occurred informed my choice to change the result, to reframe the situation as a structural problem—something I could control. Changing *my* frame to a solution-centered outcome only happened when I took responsibility for the results and stopped blaming the students.

This produced a poignant and wonderfully effective new rule: **Strategy beats bitching every time**. Whenever I feel like complaining or hear someone else complain, remembering my rule pushes me to try and figure out the right strategy to solve the problem.

With your goals in mind, you can strategize to get a better result. Without goals, you experience life as if you were adrift at sea, battered by winds and currents from all directions. It can be a longer-than-necessary, energy-wasting, bumpy ride.

Goals are the essence of who you will become, where you direct life to take you, and what you can accomplish.

I started writing down my goals in 1992 when I was thirty-eight years old. One of those—"Be mature by making the best of every situation"—has helped me transform my life by focusing on *not* taking the afore-mentioned, easy-to-complain direction.

In 1993, I penned this goal: "Write a book to help people create mature, happy, successful lives."

Although it took twenty-seven years, I've finally fulfilled that goal. Knowing I've done it gives me that spine-tingling feeling that you get when you jump into a cool pond on a hot day. And I firmly believe putting the goal on paper made it happen.

If you haven't written your goals yet, I urge you to do it. Right now. To get you started, I have a few tips and forms (worksheets A & B on pages 163 - 168). Remember, writing out your goals is an amazing tool to help you fulfill your dreams. It's not hard to get started; just jot down three or four things you would like to happen.

Don't worry about perfect goals or good writing form. Good form is important if you already know how to swim, but if you are drowning, any stroke that gets you to shore is good enough. The same applies for creating goals.

Let's think of goal setting as if we need to make it to shore. Start with a rough draft of several ideas. Later you can go back and massage those ideas into doable goals.

When I coach people on goals, I ask them to think of two or three goals in each of the following categories: spiritual, emotional, financial, physical health, work/career, family, recreation, and education/self-improvement.

After jotting down those rough ideas, they have a preliminary set of goals.

Next, I ask them to imagine themselves one year, five years, and ten years in the future. Where would they like to be?

I also ask them to envision themselves enjoying life and having fun. What would they be doing? They write those activities as goals, too.

As you follow along, think big, be bold, and don't be afraid to set goals you feel are impossible to achieve from your current situation. Many great success stories come from humble beginnings. Had you met those people well before their glory years, you might have been tempted to write them off. "They won't amount to much," you'd have thought. And you would have been wrong. Don't make that mistake · with yourself.

After gathering your thoughts and ideas, fill out the worksheets on pages 163 – 168. Consider timetables for your goals. You don't have to hold fast to a timetable, but placing your goals on a schedule helps you accomplish them.

Use Worksheet A on page 163 to house your larger set of goals in list form. Use the second form as a little sister to the first and a stepping-stone to your larger goals. On the second form, take a smaller percentage or piece of each goal as a small, first step toward accomplishing your dreams.

For instance, in writing this book I started out with a goal of writing 500 words per day. In my stepping-stone goals I listed a starter goal of 200 words per day, a number I knew I could achieve.

The first few days, I satisfied my stepping-stone goals, but not the 500-word goal. After a week or two, I easily surpassed the 200 and ended up writing 1,200 words per day for about a month. With two months of dedicated writing under my belt, I finished the entire manuscript, a great feeling of accomplishment.

My third piece of advice for goal setting is to create and foster a goal-oriented culture around yourself, starting with your family.

With my encouragement, my entire family writes their goals and we celebrate our achievements each New Year's Day, a tradition our good friend Kathy encouraged. Even the littlest children are asked to think of their goals, which we write down for them. Reviewing these years later provides rich family enjoyment.

Goal sharing unites our family. On this very special day, each of us hears the status and direction of each other's lives.

My wife's goal to have a garden (ugh!) was energized by my daughter-in-law Rory. Knowing my past aversion to farming, I wondered if life was playing with me by giving me a wife who wanted a home garden and a professional farmer for a daughter-in-law!

Granddaughter Elle wanted to write a children's book, a goal she first envisioned at five years old. I'm proud to tell you, she and I published, *The Fox Who Sneezed* in 2018—available through Barnes & Noble and local bookstores. I'm convinced that showing Elle how to conceptualize and formalize goals made the difference.

The goals *you* envision can be as simple as wanting to see your favorite singer or group in concert, or to learn photography, or to lose a few pounds (and buy a new bathing suit), or to be nicer to your mate, or to spend holidays with family. All of these are worthwhile and, when hardened into written goals, can and will help you fulfill your dreams for a better life.

It's important to physically write out your goals, not just think about them. In a curious play on words, I advise, "If it isn't written, it doesn't exist." By writing and focusing on goals, you also stimulate a process of improved thinking, which will serve you well later in life.

One of my important goals, especially as I get older, is to stay physically active. I want to make the best of whatever time is granted to me in old age, and I want to be able to engage in physical activity. I've been able to mountain bike, swim, weight lift, and run regularly for ten years now, especially since I made the goal of doing two sprint Xterra triathlons each year. *(Xterra is a three-sport activity in which you swim, mountain bike, and mountain run.)*

Instilling habits for optimal health are important. Good goals reinforce good habits. Good habits make doing the right thing easier. Bad habits work well, too, but the results are terrible. Make your steps to good health a habit reinforced by scheduled goals.

I've included a list of my personal 2018 goals on pages 161 and 162. Check those goals out to get some ideas.

SUMMARY

Set goals to improve your chance of success. Be bold. Create goals in all areas of your life with multiple perspectives (spiritual, emotional, financial, physical health, work/career, family, recreation, and education/self-improvement). Read your goals daily to help you stay focused. Involve your family, too. Their success in life is your success in life.

Action Steps to Set Goals

1. Write your goals down! If they aren't written, they won't exist.

2. Ask yourself where you want to be in one, five, and ten years. Envision specific positive results within those time frames. Examples:

   a. In one year I will be on a budget with no outstanding bills.

   b. In the next five years, I will have saved ten percent of my earnings each year.

   c. I will be enjoying a Caribbean vacation one year from today.

   d. At the end of the year, I will have learned how to ride horses.

   e. I will be a supervisor within one year.

   f. I will own my own company in five years.

3. Use a schedule. Things that get scheduled are things that get done.

4. Enjoin your family in goal setting. Ask everyone to write their goals and share them with you. Make it a team effort.

5. Develop your goals from multiple perspectives: spiritual, emotional, financial, physical health, work/career, family, recreation, and education/self-improvement.

A genius probably wouldn't

... *worry if goals aren't met right away.*
→ *Trust the process.*

... *share goals with naysayers.*
→ *Spend your energy on your goals.*

Our path forward

In Step 2, we shared how goals create a pathway for a better future and help us overcome obstacles.

In Step 3, we'll share the immense power mentors can have in your life. Finding great mentors is more difficult than you might think. You can't orchestrate the process like a symphony that's already been composed. Step 3 shows how I found my mentors—or they found me.

FIND MENTORS

Wouldn't it be great if each one of us discovered
the hidden talent in one other person?

~ Steve Kelley

Every action reverberates through the universe in ways we cannot see.

I settled into a storytelling class, wondering what the heck I was doing there. The professor, Dr. Edmund Ostrander, was a short, grumpy old bastard wearing large, round, cloudy glasses with lenses the size of baseballs. The thirty-one other students were teachers seeking master's degrees at the National Institute for Teacher Excellence at Cambridge College.

My discomfort with the idea of telling fairy tales and stories made me regret my decision. I wasn't even a teacher. What had possessed me to take this foolish course?

Yet, I had to admit, this professor, with his deep rumbling voice, had presence, the kind of presence that commanded everyone's attention.

His classroom persona was enormous, yet it hid his even bigger heart. We quickly settled into a no-niceties, get-down-to-business discussion of what was expected.

His message to us on the first day of class: You will tell stories. You will create your own story. You will be on time for classes.

I don't know why, but I liked the grumpy old bastard, perhaps because he wasn't full of himself, he didn't B.S., and he didn't sugar-coat everything in the ways I had come to expect from academic authority figures.

Importantly, he walked the talk. He had a wry, piercing humor. And, wow, could he tell poignant stories.

There was one other strikingly unusual thing about Dr. Ostrander. Hanging from a chain around his neck was a talisman, a pendant of a three-inch, grey wizard holding a crystal ball—a gift he received from an aging storyteller. It was, Dr. Ostrander explained, a high honor given to someone accomplished in the art of storytelling and had been accompanied by a poem, which Dr. Ostrander regularly recited in his high tenor voice—rich, beautiful, and booming!

This gift I send must 'ere abide,

And never, ever leave your side,

And you must seek until you find

The one who is the next in line.

And when your deed is done at last,

This talisman again must pass.

Each time he recited the poem, Dr. Ostrander inspired me. How had he made such an incredible career of teaching and storytelling?

Before I share how this grumpy old bastard changed my life, let me take you back to my second attempt at college.

Following my divorce, I needed a course correction. I was going nowhere fast. Going back to college to get a degree represented a life-line and gave me purpose in my life. I was trying to shake off the feeling of being a loser.

At first, I felt like a fish out of water at the school. I wasn't sure what I should study, or what my academic and career path should be. I had enrolled in the Portfolio Program, which allowed me to document prior learning outcomes. My goal for my portfolio was to prove my management knowledge and skills. Creating the portfolio would help me run my business and help prepare me for a new business.

With twenty-five years of business ownership experience under my belt, several of the early courses I took had a simplistic quality to them. Getting knocked around for two-and-a-half decades by hard-core, tough-negotiating general contractors and cheap, money-constrained homeowners was a far cry from the soft, un-provable theories I was being exposed to in the classroom.

I had trouble knowing what to study to maximize my investment in my education. I was keenly aware of the cost (especially my time) and the value I expected. The tuition money was coming directly out of my pocket at a time when I did not have an extra penny.

Like most students entering college, I didn't know the specific academic path to take. I struggled with studying because it pulled time away from my family and the all-too-real business concerns of supporting myself and my sons.

Often, after studying until nearly midnight, I would be up at 5 a.m. to meet and dispatch my roofing crews. Then I'd work a ten-hour day on the roof, or do administrative work or sales. After a full day, I'd have to fight traffic at rush hour on my way into Boston, scramble for a parking spot near the school, and jog to class to be on time.

One day a professor arrived forty minutes late for a 6 p.m. class. Because of how hard my day had been and what I felt was his disrespect for the effort of *my* energy and sacrifice to arrive on time, I walked out the door. Yup, I got up and walked right past the professor, in the front of the class, and out the door without saying a word.

I'm laughing as I write this, but I still remember how mad I was. I bet on the day I strode out, my fellow students could almost see steam spewing from my ears.

I dropped the class.

My goal at the time was simply to push through the college work and get a degree.

How I handled situations like the tardy professor made college a tough transition for me. But eventually I developed more tolerance and better habits. College became a better fit once I transitioned to study in the early morning hours (3-5:30 a.m.) while I juggled my other responsibilities.

My first course at Cambridge College had been with Dr. Linda Ostrander. She and her husband, Ed, had been mainstays at the college for over two decades. Linda taught her courses with intention and authenticity. I, on the other hand, wasn't a great student. She tried hard to get through to me, but I was in a bit of a funk or depression after coming through my divorce.

To help me, Linda presented a theory: Things happen in one of only three ways—by chance, by choice, or by crisis. It took a while to sink in, but slowly I realized my situation fit with this theory.

With Dr. Linda Ostrander's encouragement to reassess and rethink, I became convinced the things that had happened in my life had not been caused by chance or by crisis. My troubles, I decided, were most often caused by choice. My choice, to be precise. This concept of personal choice as the controlling factor in our outcomes is known as agency.

As I explored this new worldview of personal responsibility, I realized that, as an independent contractor, I had developed a very strong belief in my control over my destiny—or my agency. Yet when things went poorly, I conveniently let myself off the hook and whitewashed or glossed over the responsibility of my missteps as attacks on me that were out of my control.

I wasn't alone. When things went wrong on a job or with people around me, those people blamed everyone and everything but themselves. Most people don't take enough responsibility for what happens in their lives. I was no different.

Fortunately for me, Dr. Linda Ostrander didn't buy in to my resistance to take responsibility. When she questioned me about my responsibility, and received resistance and denial, she gently urged me to deeper self-examination. With her help, I created a new awareness of my role in my outcomes to uncover a better understanding of my actions.

That better understanding allowed me to improve the quality of my life. As my thinking evolved, I became more aware of my framing. And as I started to consistently use more accurate frames, I was able to work better with everyone and get better results.

With Dr. Linda Ostrander's guidance, I completed my portfolio of prior learning and entered the graduate program for management. I would go on to get a master's degree with a specialization in negotiation.

This period of my life was my chance to reboot, just like a computer needs to be re-booted when it doesn't work. To reset my life, I looked toward my internal processes to assess how each result could be traced back to actions on my part.

Even the terrible house fire, which derailed my life by various events it set into motion, could have been prevented by better decisions on my part. The faulty GFI was vulnerable to the salt spray only because of its position on the exterior wall closest to the ocean. I could have changed that, but didn't. If I had insisted on the GFI placement in a more protected place, that awful day might never have happened.

With deeper self-analysis, and because I was so intent on making over my life and getting it right, I explored the ways I had affected my outcomes. And I learned to ask myself a key question: "Was there anything I could have done to change the outcome?"

The answers to this great question allowed me to take responsibility for each thing that happened—and to honor my agency. I had now found a pathway forward to rebalance my life, re-set priorities, and most importantly to continue believing in myself. I learned to set goals as seen in Step 2.

In going through the humbling experience of rebuilding my life, I realized believing in myself seems self-evident. Yet I don't think we can reinforce this important mindset enough. You need to believe in yourself completely.

In real time, circumstances seemed to conspire to undermine me. Perhaps in your dark times, you feel that way, too. During those months of self-doubt and self-reflection, it wasn't that easy to believe in myself. Divorce, debt, and ongoing responsibilities provided lots of stress and tested the idea. Fortunately, I found some help in an unlikely place.

Storytelling.

THE MAGIC OF STORYTELLING

I was barely taking time to breathe between programs as I undertook a full course load of management courses and completed several business portfolios for credit. Within eighteen months, I received my bachelor's degree and joined a master's program for business with a specialization in negotiation.

With a focus on the narratives people use in negotiations, I decided to take a storytelling course—which was certainly not a requirement for my degree. On a hunch, I enrolled anyway.

Dr. Edmund Ostrander's storytelling class wasn't magic for me. Several students claimed it would be a gut course, a filler, an easy pass. Instead, it hit me in a weak spot I didn't know I had. Virtually everyone in the class, as teachers, had practiced speaking in front of classrooms of people, and some had practice telling stories. My anxiety increased as I witnessed their polished performances.

I was a disgruntled roofer who had never given a speech or spoken in public.

I was so embarrassed when I got up to speak in front of the group that sweat poured down my forehead, my throat constricted, and my voice wobbled and went hoarse. Self-inflicted tension caused me to forget the stories halfway through, and I couldn't stand still or meet anyone's gaze. I was truly awful.

At the four-day intensive, we attended class from 9 a.m. to 5 p.m. I bolted out each day at lunchtime to hide and lick my wounds.

Each day in class, students took turns telling stories from Jane Yolen's wonderful book, *Favorite Folktales*. The bravest and most inspired among the group told their individual, personal stories.

Dr. Ed Ostrander's fantastic ability to tell stories was in stark contrast to my own inability to tell those same stories. He taught us to start with a hook, to trust the flow, to listen with our hearts, to have a coda. He taught the many purposes of storytelling, including:

- To share knowledge, to inform about culture, to bridge cultural differences.

- To show affection, to cheer someone, to encourage, to have fun.

- To solve problems, to unify, to create common ground, to share a vision.

- To connect with people, to inspire, to motivate, to break the ice.

- To illustrate a specific point, to convince, to warn, to listen.

- To build family and group ties, to share history.

- To heal (through a cathartic telling of a difficult story).

- To stimulate discussion, to fire imaginations with new ideas and places.

The message of Dr. Ed Ostrander's class was clear: Storytelling is vital to all of us, but especially to teachers and parents. Dr. Barry Scheckley from the University of Connecticut defines learning as creating a durable and retrievable memory trace. Personal stories do that best.

Over time, I came to realize storytelling also is important in business. Most of the deals people negotiate focus on the story each side tells through their use of frames. Negotiations are a pitch-and-catch of ideas and frames that determines outcomes. But telling a story, I discovered, was more difficult than negotiating.

By the end of the class, Dr. Ed Ostrander had everyone marching to his beat—except me. On the last day as we closed out the class and filled out the teacher evaluations, everyone filed out with thank-yous and good-byes. I tried to slip out with the group, but the grumpy old bastard called me over to his desk and asked me to stay and talk.

I didn't know what to expect. I was upset with myself. I knew my performance in the class had been sub-par. I didn't know what to do about it or how to fix it. I didn't want to expend any more effort, either. My ego was bruised, and four days of torture was enough. I wanted only to escape and never come back.

I felt incompetent, and like I was a failure. Even though I had managed my own construction business for twenty years, bootstrapped myself out of the poverty I was born into, put myself and my sons through college, I couldn't get up in front of a group and tell a simple fairy tale.

When I was a child, no one had ever told me stories or given me the opportunity to tell a story; we weren't a storytelling family. In addition, I was a low self-monitor with poor social skills and especially low self-esteem after a bad divorce.

Ed told me the truth. He was good at that—the best ever. He had an unflinching ability to call it like he saw it.

"You flunked, Steve."

Of course I had.

Of all the courses one might flunk in a college curriculum, I flunked storytelling. I'd like to say that I couldn't believe it, or that I didn't deserve it, but I knew he was right. It was apparent and justified.

Ed wasn't done with me. He offered me a deal.

"You flunked, Steve, but if you'll register for my next class (four more all-day intensives), I'll give you an A for this course. I believe you could become a good storyteller."

I couldn't believe he would do that, care that much. He wanted me in his next class? He saw potential?

"Yes!" I said, impulsively, and regretted it right away. But it was too late. My fate was sealed.

So I stayed back, like in grade school, and took the course again. Of course Ed broke the rules. No one ever does that in college. You don't get a do-over in college. There's big money at play. Ed didn't care. He was all about helping people, not the bureaucracy of college.

I was a project. Ed's project. He never told me this, but I think in a comical way, he viewed me as a litmus test as to whether he could be the greatest storytelling teacher of all time. All he had to do was get me to tell one good story in front of a full class.

In the second session, I fared better as I got more familiar with the materials and a bit more comfortable speaking in front of a group.

During this time, Ed and I became very close. I would meet him before each class and carry his supplies and briefcases. We'd talk about everything—school, current events, storytelling, our kids, his life, my life. He invited me to lunch with him and his wife, Linda. And I'd help him with cleanup at the end of each class. By now Ed was seventy-three, teaching with more verve and power than professors half his age.

To be sure, Ed had a short fuse and got frustrated easily but I no longer viewed him as a grumpy old bastard.

How wrong I had been.

Instead, he had become my mentor, someone who cared deeply about making the world a better place. He cared about me. I wasn't used to that at all. Someone with his credentials who stepped into my life and cared about me was more than a novelty. It was a miracle.

I watched Ed operate. Ed didn't tolerate the dimwitted. Often, he would listen to someone for a short period, and then stop them short with an incisive, cut-to-the-bone comment. He usually picked out the errant frame in which someone was operating. He didn't tolerate B.S. at all. He was the most sharp-witted person I had ever met.

Dean of the school and a truly nice person, Jorge Cardoso, was a dear friend of the Ostranders. Their adoption of me meant Dean Cardoso also accepted the new kid on the block. Jorge and I forged what would be a lifelong relationship.

Jorge told awful stories, sometimes to the entire student body at an assembly, and Ed cringed in pain as if Jorge were burning his ears and professionally insulting them.

Here is an example of Dean Cardoso's stories:

This string goes into a soda bar and sits down on the stool. The soda jerk—that's the person behind the counter back in the day—moves over to the string and says, "Hey, we don't serve strings here. Get on out of here."

So the string gets up and goes outside and comes up with an idea. He decides to change the way he looks to get in. So he takes the end of his string and frizzes it all up, and then he ties himself in a neat knot at the waist.

He goes back into the soda bar and grabs a stool. The soda jerk looks at him closely and says, "Hey, aren't you the same string that was in here a while ago?" To which the string responds, "I'm a-frayed knot!"

Now if you are groaning and your brow is wrinkling as you try to piece together what little part of that story could possibly make it worth telling, then you have a small idea of how much pain it caused a talisman-toting storyteller.

After hearing Jorge's story, Ed would go on one of the feisty tirades that originally made me think he was a grumpy old bastard.

"What the hell kind of a joke was that? Jorge thinks he's funny. But he isn't. He's awful."

And Linda, a loving and dedicated wife, would say in her most understanding voice, "Now, Ed, go easy."

He'd scowl and growl like an angry dog, and quiet down.

I don't know what Ed saw in me. Whatever he saw had been missed by everyone else up to that point in my life. I was one lucky guy to get an opportunity to learn from such an authentic, brilliant, skilled, deeply caring professional.

When I think of Ed, I think of *Advah*—a beautiful concept in the Jewish faith—meaning ripple. Envision a giant, still, peaceful pond under a quiet sky in a closing sunset. Drop in a magic-coated pebble.

The ripple the pebble makes would touch every molecule of water, every fish, and every plant in the pond.

Ed touched so many students in his forty years of teaching. How lucky we all were in his magical *Advah*!

Our relationship, our story, didn't end when the class ended. As we closed out the class and everyone filed out after their goodbyes, Ed motioned again for me to visit. This time the grumpy old bastard told me I'd done okay ... but I could do better.

"Would you like to come to the next class and really learn storytelling well?"

Another do-over?

I was in stunned disbelief. This required some serious thought. Another investment of four long days? Another set of embarrassing attempts to learn and tell stories?

As I drove home, mulling over his offer, something changed. Something ... rippled. Storytelling had gotten under my skin.

I decided to make it my mission and goal to learn to tell stories. I didn't know it then, but this would be the best decision of my life, and would change it forever.

Ed called to check on me a couple of days before his next class. He didn't ask if I was coming. He assumed I'd be there. I wasn't sure what my role was in his plan, or why he continued to be interested in my storytelling ability (or lack of it), or why he wanted me to be in the class again. I was confused by the whole process, but Ed had sunk the hook, and I bit.

Ed told me to prepare something about listening skills for the class.

I was reading Stephen Covey's acclaimed The *7 Habits of Highly Effective People* and was motivated by his view of listening, which he calls The Magical Skill. Magical, because it is an other-centered activity, which uniquely benefits both speaker and listener by stimulating them, connecting them, and—in so doing—building trust, awareness, and understanding.

Challenged, I wrote my small lesson plan as I had observed Ed do many times in the previous classes.

Ed called on the morning of class and asked me to delay my arrival until thirty minutes after the class was to start. I didn't like being late, because it made me stand out. I didn't know what Ed was up to, but I complied.

When I arrived, Ed introduced me as his assistant. My head swiveled like a bobble-headed corkscrew. I couldn't believe my ears.

"Steve has prepared a lesson on listening," he told the class of twenty-eight teachers. "I'll turn the time over to him."

All of them knew more about a lesson plan by their first year of college than I did at this moment. Still, I was determined to do my best. I wasn't going to let this storytelling thing get the better of me.

The experience was awful. Unlike Ed, I had no stage presence. Zero. The class took a short recess after I concluded the lesson. Ed pulled me aside and asked how I thought I'd done. I told him that I wasn't good at all.

"You'll do better next time."

I was learning that every stumble would be a win.

Ed showed me that if you believed in yourself and didn't give up, you could improve. What a powerful message. Take your failures in stride and keep working at improving. Curiously, at this point, I hadn't realized Ed had taken me under his wing as his protégé and was grooming me. I was oblivious.

He was right. I did do better the next time. As I continued to help Ed with his classes, leading the lessons got easier. (Curiously, almost like a career forecast, I would later teach classes in effective listening at Curry College. More on that later.)

As we concluded the weekend and gave assignments for the following weekend, students came to me for advice on their assignments. Since I had been repeating this course, I knew what advice to give. They would have been surprised to learn I was there only because I flunked out several months earlier.

Ed asked if I could give him some help the following weekend, too. I nodded my agreement.

I was starting to feel more comfortable in the academic setting but the feeling was fleeting. Wednesday evening, Ed phoned.

His voice was strained. "Steve, I have to go into the hospital in Houston this weekend."

My brows shot up. "What do you mean Ed? Is this a joke?"

"Steve! I've had a heart attack. I need your help."

This was serious. My throat tightened. "Whatever you need, Ed. What can I do for you?"

"Steve, you have to go in and teach the class this weekend."

With panic in my voice, I frantically refuted the idea. "Ed, I just can't do that. I'm not a teacher. I'm not qualified. Linda can do it. Put Linda on the phone!"

Ed coughed, and coughed again. "Steve," he said in a hoarse whisper, "she won't leave my side." His voice trailed off, even weaker. "Admin will take the course from me, Steve. Too many instructors want to teach it. I developed this course. It's my blood. You owe me, Steve, and you have to do this!"

I gulped. "Jesus, Ed. I don't think I can."

Irate now, he sputtered in a raspy but forceful voice, "Yes! You can! Why do you think I brought you along? I knew you had it in you. You have to do this for me!"

Now he was *really* being a grumpy old bastard. He had been through hell, and I didn't want to challenge him, upset him, add to his distress.

Queasiness spread through my stomach, but Ed was my friend. I nodded. "Okay, Ed. I'll do my best."

I couldn't imagine that this would have a good ending.

I spent the next forty-eight hours reviewing my notes, making handouts, and preparing on little sleep. I did owe Ed. And I was determined to teach the class for him.

On Saturday morning, I told the students Dr. Ostrander was undergoing triple bypass surgery. We would have to proceed without him. No one objected. (Had I thought they would?) We followed the syllabus and the routine Ed had developed and used countless times before. As a whole, the class was incredible. Their stories were riveting. The challenge of learning without their professor provided a laser focus on the material.

By 4 p.m. Sunday, the last day of the intensive, the students had become a team of dedicated, masterful storytellers. They gathered for a meeting and asked for private time.

"Would you mind leaving the room, Mr. Kelley?"

I did as I was asked.

Evaluation forms had just been delivered in an envelope by the dean's office. As I waited outside the classroom, I observed one of the students slipping into the dean's office. They were requesting—I would learn later—two sets of evaluations: one for the first half of the course with Dr. Ostrander and one for the second half of the course with me. Although a bit anxious, I was at peace knowing I had given my best effort.

Later, I phoned Ed in Houston. His voice sounded stronger. The bypass surgery was a success! Relief surged through me. I let him know I had completed the course for him and now we would have to wait and see how the evaluations went.

On Tuesday, my office phone rang.

Ed's voice practically boomed into my ear. "Steve, my friend at the dean's office got back to me about the evaluations."

My heart pounded, but I tried to ignore it.

"You're in, Steve." Ed sounded gleeful.

"In? What do you mean?" I was perplexed.

"Steve, the school wants you to be my assistant and teach with me. They are going to pay you as an assistant while I recuperate."

Not in a million years would I have guessed I would be an assistant professor. Or that I would teach the subject that, just a short time ago, I loathed for exposing my weaknesses. Make no mistake; this wasn't a shock just to me. No one who knew me would've thought I would be a professor of anything. Storytelling had changed my life.

I had found a mentor and a champion, someone who would help me succeed. We would help each other. I would not fail if Dr. Edmund Ostrander had anything to do with it.

> *How wonderful the world would be if each of us discovered the hidden talent in one other person.*

SUMMARY

Seek mentors who share your values. Life takes us on strange paths. Follow your intuition. Be willing to let go. When you find someone willing to invest in you, pay it back: invest in him or her. Being mentored involves work on the part of the mentee. Offer something of value to a mentor.

Make yourself the best you can be so that great mentors can find you.

Action Steps to Find Mentors

1. Be honest with yourself. Learn who you are. Think about someone you admire. Do a character analysis on them. Who are they? What are their traits? What do they do? What philosophers do they admire? Ask those same questions of yourself.

2. Push yourself to be better and to develop your character. Believe in YOU! That person will attract the right mentor.

3. Make a list of things you would like to explore. List anything you are curious about: art, theater, dancing, writing, sports, yoga, gardening.

4. Join an online or neighborhood club. Volunteer for a worthwhile cause. Pick something new to learn. Enroll in a course that inspires your curiosity.

5. Find people doing good things for the community. Interview them for ideas and inspiration.

6. If you are not satisfied with the environment you are in, or that environment isn't healthy for any reason, find ways to create the distance you need to move into new environments.

A genius probably wouldn't

... reach for a rotting branch.

→ *Genius thinking: Reach higher for great mentors in good environments.*

Our path forward

In Step 3, we shared the wonderful power of great mentors.

In Step 4, we'll focus on creating optimal physical and mental health to give ourselves the best chances at great futures.

TAKE GREAT CARE OF YOUR BODY

If you don't take care of your body, where are you going to live?

~ Kobi Yamada

Fill your actions with love.

It's a typical Saturday morning at 5:30 a.m., and I'm loading my mountain bike into my pick-up truck and getting ready to meet Luis (fifty-four), Stuart (seventy), and Dave (fifty-three). The four of us will ride bikes for two hours in Blue Hills Reservation today. My tongue will be dragging, as I chase these guys from the back of the pack. I just try to keep up.

Luis has run 118 marathons, Stuart is the New England Xterra triathlon champion in his age group for eight years running, and Dave has just completed sixteen sprint triathlons, even though he has been fighting cancer for the last five years.

These guys know how to care for their bodies. It is important work, and they don't let obstacles get in their way. To illustrate, I'll let them share their stories. (You'll hear from Stuart in Step 6). But first, here's my wife, Susan, sharing her perspective on how to take care of your body.

Susan's Story

I just woke up. It's 6 a.m. (argggh). I hear the garage door shut as Steve leaves for his morning biking exercise with his friends. If I can't go back to sleep, I'll probably get on the treadmill for an hour and then start my day. My husband is proud of my disciplined approach to health. People can't guess my age and are often off by twenty years.

I'm a physician assistant with a background in geriatric care and internal medicine. In my profession, I see too many people in poor health who have lost their independence because they did not take care of themselves well.

During my twenty-year career, I've learned three things to help you create optimal physical health: exercise, healthy eating, and understanding the mind-body connection.

When I was young, Mom and Dad made every meal from scratch. We had fresh fruit, vegetables, fresh salads, and delicious homemade spaghetti sauce. Chain restaurants were at a minimum, and restaurant eating was a special treat, not a convenience. There were no microwave ovens.

I remember when the TV dinner was first introduced. Packaged in aluminum containers, they were a treat, and we were excited to taste each new replacement meal. Little did we know we were on the precipice of overall declining health and a steep decline from natural foods to unhealthy chemically-preserved, fat-sabotaged, artery-clogging salt-and-sugar-laced food.

Fortunately, I was normal weight, but the love of all-things-bad-that-tasted-good had begun for me and the rest of my generation. Later in life, as I continued my food and medical education, I learned how much nutrition, eating behaviors, stress, where and how you live, and psychology affect our mind-body connection.

I discovered the unnatural convenience foods—food bullets—we had learned to eat are addictive and adversely affect our health. Metaphorically speaking, we are shooting ourselves in the foot when we eat this junk.

In my thirties, I noticed the food bullets starting to hit their target: me. In response, I exercised at several women's gyms (Gloria Stevens, Women's World, etc.). I tried to research what to eat. Unfortunately, the consensus on foods changed year-to-year depending on who wrote the articles. Sometimes salt was bad for you. Sometimes fat was bad. Then fat was necessary, and sugar was bad, but it could be good. Butter was bad. Margarine was better. It was—and is—still confusing.

I dieted to be healthy and to keep my figure. Size eight was my goal. Size six was a memory.

I tried a bunch of popular diets: cabbage soup, grapefruit, no carbs, etc. Rigid diets didn't work for me. I realized I needed to maintain a pattern of eating and exercise to maintain my weight.

I found friends who liked to walk. We talked, shared, consoled, cajoled, laughed, cried, educated, and bonded. I stayed active. Eventually I found a better way to eat. I watched what I ate and restricted salt, fat, sugar, and bread, and I ate smaller portions. What you eat and how much you eat really matters.

Sadly, we have learned that the basic four food groups taught in our schools (milk, meat, fruits and vegetables, and grains) were lobbied into school curriculums by huge agricultural and food companies, with little emphasis on science and research. Powerful meat and dairy industries fought against a newly proposed Eating Right Pyramid in the early 1990s. Chemicals crept into our diet, and research on the effects of introducing growth hormones to fatten livestock and increase production were discounted as our food became less and less healthy.

When I was in my forties, I went back to college to obtain a degree in physician assistant studies. I sat on the train in and out of the city, sat all day in school, and then sat at home doing homework. With little time for the gym, exercise, or for cooking healthy food, and with lots of added stress, I gained weight and felt sluggish. Even someone as health-focused as I am can have trouble staying healthy.

While studying nutrition and the mind-body connection, I learned the you-are-what-you-eat principle: garbage in, garbage out. I came to understand that knowing why you eat what you do—and when you choose to eat it—matters, along with education about nutrition as well as peer input from parents, family, friends, and colleagues. I knew I had to return to what Mom and Dad practiced: eat fresh salads; cook from scratch; limit fast food; and limit convenience products, which are loaded with fat, salt, sugar, and chemicals. I worked hard to learn about food, portion control, and lifestyle choices.

Since becoming a physician assistant, I have focused on health maintenance and disease prevention. Unlike the way it is delivered today in hospitals everywhere, medical care needs to be thought of as an integrative process. It should focus on prevention, not just treatment after a disease has occurred, when reversing negative conditions is nearly impossible.

Every day I meet people who have not taken care of their bodies, or people whose health changed by crisis or lack of control. They are overweight, with joint pain, high blood pressure, high cholesterol, diabetes, and cardiac problems. Some are diabetics but don't know which foods have carbohydrates or sugar; some have congestive heart failure and leg swelling but don't know which foods contain high amounts of sodium. There is no magic bullet, pill, or surgery to make these people better.

A better prescription would be for all of us to learn to act preemptively on behalf of our bodies. I eat lots of no-salt vegetable soups, fruits, and salads every week. We only get one body, and food is a big part of the path to cultivating a healthy body and preventing disease.

With my family and especially my grandchildren, I encourage a healthy lifestyle. Babies are born with a relatively clean slate, meaning toxins have not built up in their bodies. If we can focus the next generations on organic and natural products in everything from food, clothing, furniture, cosmetics, and even toiletries, they can avoid ingesting harmful chemicals into their bodies.

Whether for parents, day-care providers, teachers, or children, education about eating foods with less salt, fat, and sugar will improve their futures. Macaroni and cheese might be easy, but it isn't healthy.

In my fifties, I attended a presentation by Dan Buettner about Blue Zones, special areas in the world where people live longer. Dan's research showed that physical location, activities, food habits, and the people with whom you associate matter. His message resonated with me. He suggested that living near healthy food sources and surrounding yourself with like-minded friends and family affects the mind-body connection—which can translate into longevity.

The habits we form as we mature can have lasting beneficial effects or detrimental effects. Buettner emphasized good habits and strongly advanced the idea of having purpose in your life and a strong social network, good people to talk to and with.

We live near a park with hiking, walking, and biking trails and a pond for swimming and kayaking. This environment does for my family what Dan Buettner suggests: It promotes exercise and healthy living. There are always friends and family around to talk to and learn from.

In summary, with my full medical experience and education, I can firmly advocate that the most important thing you can do for yourself and your family is to respect and take care of your body and your health. You will feel better, stay at a healthy weight, look better, and allow your body's organs to function optimally. In doing so, you will maintain your independence for as long as you can.

In addition, find a strong purpose. Start a home garden or join a CSA (community supported agriculture) program or volunteer at a farm. Eat organic foods. Read labels. Research. Limit empty calories and junk food. Watch your salt intake. No smoking. No drugs. Limit alcohol.

Surround yourself with quality, like-minded people who are good influences and who can encourage you and help you to honor your most precious asset: your body. Venerate your vessel and you will sail everywhere!

Finding great friends who share your values is crucial to building the habits of a healthy body and enhancing the mind-body connection.

I've tried to adhere to my wife's advice, especially when it comes to exercise. Several years back while riding my mountain bike at Borderland State Park near my house, I came upon a fellow running at a great pace, so much so I had trouble keeping up with him. As I pulled alongside Luis, I saw he was barely out of breath while I was huffing and puffing up the hill.

"Geez, nice running, dude!" I congratulated.

He smiled in acknowledgment, and we slowed to a nice talking pace as we crested the hill. I wanted to know how he had put himself in such great shape. As we talked, we felt an instant bond. Over time, we became great friends.

It turned out Luis was from Linares, Mexico, and was an experienced marathoner—110 marathons! Surprisingly, with all those races accomplished, Luis was a down-to-earth person. His stamina was amazing, but he also had unique points of view unlike those of anyone I had ever met.

Luis's Story

Today is Monday, March 5, 2018, and I'm on a flight back to Boston from my 118th marathon—the Woodlands Texas Marathon.

I'm fifty-four. When I run now, it's ugly. I'm not in the shape I should be, and I struggle to finish each race. Yet I still love doing it.

People ask why I pay the entry fees and travel thousands of miles from my family, job, and friends, just to beat up my body.

My answer is complicated. Most people like me have some sort of obsessive-compulsive disorder (OCD). Running makes me uncomfortable enough to keep my OCD in check. With a running routine, even back at age twenty-two, I could feel myself coping better than anyone around me. Wait. There's more.

I believe we live in a society that doesn't honor pain. I view pain tolerance like muscle building and weightlifting. As you experience pain, you develop strength and counter-resistance to the pain itself.

The greatest successes in life require great sacrifices. In knowing pain and handling it as something to be respected, not ignored or avoided, we can better prepare for the bumps and bruises life delivers. Call it Pain Training.

Society and the medical community don't view pain the same way I do. Instead, they encourage us to avoid pain and mask it at every opportunity with liquor, medication, and drugs of all types.

Anesthetizing pain doesn't serve us well. Pain educates. We need to know pain, not erase it from our experience. It might sound odd and masochistic, but I'm not a masochist. I don't enjoy pain.

I know that to get great gains in life, you need to make great sacrifices. That's part of Pain Training. Of course people need to be mindful to not overdo it.

Buddhists hold the concept of *Tapaysa*, which can be translated to self-suffering.

Tapaysa gives me the canvas on which to paint my experiences and the impressions life makes on me. *Tapaysa*, within the sport of running, improves my coping skills and builds depth. It is the perfect outlet for all of the scratches and cuts people inflict in everyday life. It helps me to have better judgment.

Physically, I can feel myself strain to maintain my brain's production of the precious protein that turns pain into the touted runner's high.

As I get older, I still want to improve, but the objective now is more of a mind-body-soul connection. I am less interested in competing and comparing myself with others. This frees me from attempting to pin down an entry number or qualification. Often, the lonelier the run, the better.

This holds true except when Steve or one of the others in our group sends a harassing email with a tempting invitation to punish ourselves on another run or ride.

On late Friday nights when my wife Gaby hears the pings coming from my cellphone, she rolls her eyes. She knows it's my friends wanting me to accompany them.

"I thought you do this to stay sane," she reminds me. "There is nothing sane with that bunch."

With running and exercise, I've grown from the little-bit-off kid who ran back and forth in Linares, Mexico, to a successful person with deep, well-thought-out convictions about how a life should be run (pun intended).

As I watch my three beautiful daughters grow into great adults, I know my running has helped me gain the depth to counsel them in every event in their lives.

Whether I do Ironman events or ultra-marathons of one hundred miles, the willingness to suffer is the core of how I experience life. Pain provides a base lens to cope.

Dave's Story

No one embraced health and a no-excuses mentality better than Dave DeSantis with his iron will and heart of gold. No one I've ever met was tougher than Dave. His focus on diet, training, and mind-body health was unparalleled. I'm honored to have known Dave. He lived life to the fullest and exemplified *carpe diem* until he passed on June 5, 2017, after a heroic battle with cancer.

Dave did sixteen sprint triathlons in 2016, the last year of his life. His wife, Kathy, was a rock who supported him in a way no legacy or any heroine could ever match. What a team!

I met Dave in 2008. I was his recovery buddy. After cancer treatments, he couldn't go as fast as he wanted, so I'd be the slow guy who paced him. Actually, I couldn't keep up with him. He was amazing.

On those rides, he was always modest about relating his accomplishments, even when I pushed him to brag a little. I wanted to know his secret to success.

It was attitude.

Dave wouldn't let a rock, a trail, a river, or even cancer beat him in a race. So you can see for yourself the heart of a champion. Here is an excerpt from his Xterra Albay report in the Philippines in 2015. (Notice the framing he used.)

"The cycle of battling this tumor has now become a routine. I'll go on the BRAF medication (which is keeping the tumors from growing) and after the thirteenth to fifteenth day of being on the medication, the side effects kick in: fevers, vomiting, diarrhea, headaches, mouth sores, and joint swelling. Then it's necessary to cycle off the drugs in order to get the side effects under control. The good news is that we now know generally what to expect and when to expect it to occur.

Happily, I was recovered enough on the day of the flight to sit still for the twenty-six-hour flight. We flew through Tokyo and arrived in Manila on 1/25. We had a night in Manila then on to Legazpi the next day. Legazpi is a city of 200,000 people located 250 miles south of Manila. The city and region are known for the Mayon Volcano that rises up from the ocean to 7500'; it is an active volcano that is truly impressive.

The Xterra course begins on the eastern side of the volcano with a swim in the Pacific, then biking up the volcano through rice fields, jungle, lava beds, rivers, villages, etc., and finishes on the western side of the volcano with a run up a huge riverbed of streams, volcanic sand, and rice fields.

The swim is a triangle: swim out from the shore at a forty-five-degree angle to the first buoy then turn right and swim parallel to the shore then another right turn and forty-five-degree line back to the shore.

I plan to run up the beach 100-150 meters then dive in to cut down the angle to the first buoy. I'm sure every other athlete is thinking the same thing. As the start nears, all of the race marshals are pushing the athletes down the beach and all the athletes are pushing up the beach to get in the best position possible for the start. The gun goes off: Everyone sprints left up the beach. At about 20 meters, a bunch of pros dive in and start swimming. I keep running and running, and running. At about 100 meters, it's just me and one other guy running and everyone else is in the water.

The other guy is Maurico Mendez. He's nineteen years old, from Mexico, and an amazing athlete. At 150 meters, we both dive in and start to swim. Mendez flies by me and I'm now second-guessing this strategy. Then I start breathing on my right side and see that Mendez and I are ahead of the entire field. By the time we hit the first turn buoy, Mendez is in the lead and I'm in the middle of the pros. The next leg is parallel to the beach, then a right turn and back to the shore. I exit the water in under twenty-two minutes, a record for me.

The gifts keep coming: The clouds are thick, I had a great swim, and I'm finally on my bike! The first twelve kilometers are all uphill. The nutrition goes in nicely, and I get my first downhill. Things are starting to flow; this bike course was made for me. The technical sections are a blast, the loose lava sand is slowing my competitors, and I now realize that all the time I spent pre-riding the course is really paying off.

I know exactly where I am, what's around the next corner, and I'm feeling really confident about the conditions. The only concern is the water buffalo; they are everywhere along the course and they are tied to trees with long ropes. If you're flying down the course and spook them, they bolt, and if they are on one side of the trail and the tree is on the other side, you get clotheslined. No issues for me; all of the animals are cooperating. I think the pros in front of me have spooked and settled the animals.

About two miles from T2 (Transition 2) the sun comes out. The last mile of the bike is through rice fields, streams, and lava rock. I get off the bike, get my running shoes and umbrella.

The run was painfully slow; the sun was out; it was hot; and running up hill in loose sand with wet sneakers made it miserable. But miserable is good! It slowed the competition and made it easier for me to maintain my position in relation to the field. After we hit the top elevation on the run and turned down, things got better. A few clouds shaded me, and the run got a bit more technical.

Dave finished first in his age group (again). He and his niece, Rachel, attended the Xterra World Championships in Hawaii.

SUMMARY

Susan's, Luis's, and Dave's stories are the stories of champions, people who maturely make the best of their lives. They've become champions by thinking well and venerating their bodies. Each of them understands Tapaysa, which allows them to endure a healthy amount of self-suffering, pain, and sacrifice to have a great mind-body-soul connection.

Action Steps to Take Great Care of Your Body

1. Find friends who understand the importance of a healthy body.

2. Make time for exercise. Do any exercise that gets you active. Make it a habit. Start at a pace at which you are comfortable, and then build more activities like walking your dog, swimming, running, biking, yoga, stretching, weightlifting, or bird watching.

3. Eat healthy. Let food taste like the food it is. We need to relearn what a carrot or a mushroom or a pepper actually tastes like. Flavoring food with additives (salt) is overrated.

4. Get rid of soda. Cut down on caffeine, sugar, and salt, too.

5. Start a home garden or get a farm share.

6. Drink lots of water and no-calorie drinks.

7. Enhance the mind-body-soul connection by adding endurance exercise.

A genius probably wouldn't...

... *think that aging will serve him well if he isn't in shape.*
Life plays hardball at unexpected times.

... *take the escalator or elevator.*
→ **Genius thinking: Climb the stairs.**

Our path forward

In Step 4, we learned the importance of great friends with good health habits to help us care for our bodies and create physical and mental well-being. We explored ways to enhance the mind-body-soul connection.

In Step 5, Embrace Conflict, we'll talk about how each of us can handle the roadblocks we face as we move through life. We'll talk about strategies to deal with conflict and make the best of every situation.

EMBRACE CONFLICT

Out beyond the ideas of right and wrong, there is a field.
I will meet you there.
~ Rumi, 13th Century Persian Poet

Imagine a rabbit pulling a magician out of a hat.
How could it happen?

When I argue with my wife, Susan, it's because we care about each other, we are both stubborn, and we both want to be right all the time. (I lose most of these battles.)

My favorite trick to end our disagreement is to simply stop, walk outside to the porch, and ring the doorbell. It's not a self-imposed time-out, although it has the same good effect. When she opens the door (hopefully), I apologize for my role in our verbal battle.

My apology goes like this: "I'm sorry for my role in this argument." That's it. I don't offer any excuses or justifications. The apology is short, sweet, and simple. I've figured out that fighting isn't worth the precious time we are spending.

This is a winning formula for both of us. As soon as the doorbell rings, the oddity of me reentering my own house after being with her a minute before prompts my wife—who recognizes it's time for both of us to take a new direction. Even though she wins most arguments, with this trick I win, too.

Let me explain. Because we are competitive (like most couples), we have lots of opportunities to disagree. The doorbell trick becomes a contest. Each new disagreement turns into a race.

Sometimes at the same exact moment, my wife and I realize how ridiculous it is that we are fighting. We stop in unison. We rush to the door, bumping into each other as we attempt to get out of the door first to ring the doorbell. Hitting the button becomes a symbolic prize, great satisfaction for the person who gets there first.

Racing to ring the bell has become a ritual and indicates our will-ingness to do the smart thing. A simple apology after the bell is all that it takes and triggers the re-set we both need.

Try it someday with your partner. See which one of you figures it out first. It becomes a fun way to manage, escape, and end arguments, especially with those you love. This useful tool builds the good habit of de-escalating verbal spars that aren't worth having. (When you make up, that can be great, too.)

We know that whoever stepped out of the controlling effect of the fight first, and figured out that peace-making is better than fighting creates a win for both of us. We've handled the conflict well and often end up laughing and getting along much better.

Like most people, we often fight over silly stuff.

Whether the toilet paper is replaced in the pull-down or lift-up position doesn't matter—as long as someone replaces it. Whether the grass is cut on Tuesday or Friday also doesn't matter. Which shelf the tea and coffee go on doesn't matter. All of us have fights over stuff like this all the time, and that's the point: We need to be good at handling conflicts, from the silly to the serious. Poor conflict management is a time-suck we can ill afford. It's important to prevent as many silly conflicts as you can, and de-escalate the serious ones.

Conflict is ever present in our lives, from cradle to grave. From the moment we gasp our first breath of air, screaming in shock and surprise, conflict is the common denominator. How you handle it determines the outcome of your life.

As we grow up, to keep us safe and save time, our parents routinely tell us what to do: *Go to bed! Brush your teeth. Put a jacket on. Shut the door!* This shortcut control mechanism (direct commands) is a great time saver during our formative years but actually causes conflict as we mature. Direct commands to adults are counter-productive and create contention.

For instance, when you are chilly, you might say to your partner (who is more warm-blooded), "Turn the heat up to 74. It's cold in here." A far better tool to achieve your preferred outcome would be to create options: "It's a little chilly in here. Do you want to turn the heat up, or would you rather I grab a blanket?" Options empower by offering choices, a winning formula to avoid unnecessary conflict.

I'm not advocating that you totally avoid conflict. In fact, successful people embrace conflict because they know that conflict, if handled well, produces great results and often offers opportunity for self-improvement.

Each time we de-escalate conflict, halt or shorten needless arguments, we maintain our dignity, save precious time, and find hope. Conflict is a golden opportunity to take responsibility for our actions and recognize the part we played in the situation.

My Bike Story

On the day of the Big Favor, I rode my $900 mountain bike to work. It was a beautiful bike—a silver twenty-seven-gear Gary Fisher brand with disc brakes, great traction tires, and a soft, comfortable seat. On a six-mile ride to work, I detoured for some trail riding and arrived later than planned. After quickly parking my bike in the lobby below my office, I hustled upstairs to get some work done. When I returned about an hour later, my bike was gone.

Of course I was angry and swore up a storm. But I knew deep inside that playing the victim role was not going to bring my bike back. I discovered a great conflict management tool when I asked myself, "What could I have done to change the outcome?" I knew the answer: Lock the bike!

With that acknowledgment, I dropped my role as victim by stopping the Blame Game—faulting others for *my* deficiency: an unsecured bike. Recognizing my culpability made me ready to make the necessary changes in my behavior for a better outcome. As it turns out, the thief did me a Big Favor by teaching me an important lesson.

Importantly, going forward, when I use that "magic" question—"What could I do/have done to change the outcome?"—I get answers to help me reduce confusion and diagnose the sources, causes, and potential remedies to any issue.

In this case, the effect was immediate: I vowed to secure my possessions at all times so they wouldn't be stolen. I've never had a bike stolen again.

By questioning my motives and roles, I am able to quickly assess the conflict and move on to potential fixes, skills that help me as well as my conflict partners.

Conflict partners. Did you catch this unique frame I use?

In her powerful book, *The Chalice and the Blade*, Riane Eisler writes, "You cannot stand in the corner of a round room." Her prescient observation reminds us that there is no escaping our roles in conflict. When we fight with others, we are intimately connected along the lines of our disagreements. We are in it together. To get the best result, we must care about our antagonists.

Each time we identify the actions we took, or didn't take, that created the conflict, we improve our skill of conflict management and become a more effective partner in our relationships. After shouldering responsibility for my actions in "The Case of the Stolen Bike," I developed a habit of turning each conflict into a win by learning from the experience.

Let's use my stolen bike episode to understand conflict better and outline ways we can operate better in conflict situations.

> ***Conflict, in its simplest form, is the release of stored energy.***

An apt analogy is a compressed wire spring waiting to be released for an intended effect. Equally so, our past experiences can be compressed feelings, byproducts that trigger the release of our tempers. Our accusations. Our blame.

Often we don't anticipate the energy being released, but it happens organically when we argue or fight. The energy of a fight (loaded from prior unresolved events) is maintained (in our memories and feelings) or compressed further (coiled into a tighter spring)—waiting for release.

Whoever stole my bike might have been thinking, *What stupid person leaves a bike like this unlocked? Obviously, money is nothing to him. If I hadn't been fired, I'd have money to burn, too. He deserves to have his bike stolen.*

If we explore the energy released in this theft, we clearly see a person who hasn't had good training and lives a life of scarcity. When we analyze and understand the motives and thought processes behind the action, we are pointed toward the theory of behavioral consistency. My bike thief simply acted in accordance with the environment in which he grew up.

Behavioral consistency suggests if you or I were born in that person's shoes with that person's influences, we'd probably steal the bike, too.

Awareness and greater understanding of negative influences in people's lives is essential to understanding and making sense of conflict. Even though my own thoughts were, *People shouldn't steal my things*, the theory of behavioral consistency allows me to create an option for how this person was patterned into his behavior by his past.

Those kinds of options provide a more balanced view so we don't escalate conflicts needlessly. If everyone intensified every conflict and retaliated instead of finding alternative forgiving responses, we'd live in a graceless world where an eye-for-an-eye would make everyone blind.

I never saw my Gary Fisher bike again. But the thief left me with valuable lessons: He taught me to drop the Blame Game, take responsibility for my possessions—and my choices. He taught me to reframe my antagonists as conflict partners. He taught me to "look beyond" in order to understand motive and cause.

I was able to move on quickly from my stolen bike episode because I accepted my part in the problem and didn't demonize the person who stole my bike. It didn't mean I approved of his behavior. It happened. I got over it.

By moving past the conflict, I got on with my life.

To disengage from those harmful and limiting forceful behaviors we encounter, we can use the framework I've developed. COOCEOO (pronounced Koo-chee-oh) is an acronym for:

1. Create Options

2. Offer Choices

3. Empower Others and Ourselves

Like the three-legged chair supporting the person in the illustration to the left, these three action choices are a toolkit to support and respect others. COOCEOO facilitates a total paradigm shift to help you handle conflict—whether small like changing the temperature in a room or bigger like my stolen bike.

When you succeed in business primarily by force of will as I have, it is critical to recognize that there are limits to what you can accomplish by force. I was amazed to realize how much more could be accomplished by changing my mindset, creating options, and offering choices.

COOCEOO altered my business habits, made me more efficient, and opened new doors as I adopted its wisdom.

I test-drove empowering phrases like "Is it possible you could work this Saturday?" or "Do you think you might be able to do this?" or "What day works for you?" as replacements for more standard, restrictive phrases like "We are working this Saturday." or "Thursday and Friday are open. I'd like to get your job done then."

The elements of COOCEOO provide the ABCs of effective interactive skills:

(A)nalytical tools

(B)ehavioral tools

(C)ommunication tools

When you (A)nalyze a conflict situation, you can ask whether or not the participants created options for each other. Did the partner's (B)ehavior limit or create options? And did the (C)ommunication used reflect whether options were being created or whether they were limited?

For example, in a simple exchange with a co-worker who asked for feedback about a recently prepared memo, Marly might say, "Hi, Sue. Would you look at this memo?"

Sue, who is late for a meeting, scans the memo, immediately notices a misspelling and hands it back saying, "Ther-rapy is spelled wrong."

She is unaware that she has just insulted Marly, who feels unappreciated for the hours she spent on the graphics and collecting a send-to list.

If, instead, Marly had utilized COOCEOO, she might have asked Sue, "Is it convenient for you to look at this memo now?"

Sue might have responded, "It would be better if I could review it this afternoon. Would that be okay with you?"

With this option-creating, analytical framework and mindset, conflict is less easily introduced in interactions and more easily de-escalated.

Renowned conflict author Daniel Dana, Ph.D., describes conflicts in three escalating stages: blips, clashes, and crises. By creating options, we can prevent blips from becoming clashes, and prevent clashes from becoming crises. Just as importantly, we can utilize options to de-escalate crises down to clashes, clashes down to blips, and blips down to mutually productive exchanges.

When we encounter conflict in relationships, we have choices. We can repair the relationship, build the relationship, or close the relationship based on what we think is best for us.

In the courses I teach, people are often surprised by the idea that you can close a relationship. For reasons I can't explain, people keep existing relationships going, even when the relationships are detrimental and cause significant discomfort.

It's okay to close a relationship that isn't working for you. Be firm and kind when you do. Keep in mind, most likely you can open that relationship later if you both would like. If not, lesson learned. Take responsibility and move on.

COOCEOO is extremely important when you meet people for the first time. The options you create (or limit) with this framework will impact and determine the lasting impression you make.

Whether you are at a job interview or in a workplace, engaged in a buy or sell contract, attending a social or family event, creating options will have a profound effect on your future.

Conversely, when we do not utilize an option-creation mindset—by intentionally or unintentionally limiting options, denying choices and disempowering others, we subsequently disempower ourselves.

Options are definitely gifts worth giving.

Consider another important concern in conflict: How we handle information or views that oppose our own view. Often we are abrupt and can't wait to disagree when confronted with disconfirming evidence— ideas that contradict our thinking. People who embrace disconfirming evidence, instead of rejecting differences, get along better with others.

One thing I shouldn't leave out in my advice about handling conflict is to understand and honor feelings. Feelings matter. It's easy to hurt people and unwise to do so.

When our actions or words cause harm to someone's feelings, we have regret and feel helpless—with good reason. Lashing out can cause intense hurt in unpredictable directions—both for ourselves and for the person we hurt.

You can't change how people feel. Feelings are like elusive shadows shaped and trapped by prior experiences in people's lives. All you can do is honor their feelings, good or bad.

Often people form their views and use frames based on their feelings from bad experiences. You've probably heard their fatalistic predictions: "What goes around, comes around." "If people haven't disappointed you, be patient. They will."

These negative maxims evidence deep hurt. Excellent conflict management can ease their sense of helplessness.

To break the curse, we should confront conflict and sharpen our conflict skills continually.

Here are my Top Ten Tools for Conflict Management:

10. Be consistent and patient. Good systems reinforce themselves.

9. Be tactful. Feelings matter.

8. Pull together with your conflict partner, or you will pull apart.

7. Use a mantra: *Stay calm. Keep your eyes, mind, and soul open.*

6. Listen deeply. Liberate yourself from your own thinking.

5. Reward rule-breakers in your life.

4. Confront conflict tirelessly.

3. Frame conflict as an opportunity. Through conflict, life twists us to its purposes and reshapes us to survive.

2. Leave blame at home—where it belongs.

1. Don't avoid conflict. Embrace it. Conflict is pure gold.

SUMMARY

Conflict has high value because it highlights the work we need to do to improve ourselves to become more successful. We learned that letting go is more important than winning. We learned to create options, to empower others and ourselves.

Some frames for conflict are: It's not what happens to you, it's how you handle it. Leave the past where it belongs.

When we employ great conflict tools, we can turn conflict into a steppingstone for a better life.

Action Steps to Embrace Conflict

1. Take timeouts when you feel yourself getting angry or tense.

2. Use anabolic energy to guide your actions (energy that is intended to be constructive).

3. Embrace failures for what they can teach you.

4. Know that it's not what happens to you that counts; it's how you handle what happens that counts.

5. Use a mantra: Stay calm. Keep your eyes open – mind and soul too. Be very aware.

6. Take responsibility for your part in conflict. You played a part in its creation.

7. Find time to reflect, slow the pace, and determine more appropriate frames.

8. Break your regimen. If you are working, go home from work early occasionally. Build a reserve to face conflict when it happens.

A genius probably wouldn't...

... *be a Chicken Little.*

→ **Genius thinking: The sky is not falling. Ever.**

... *banish his opponents!*

→ **Let them save face. Be an Aikido warrior, responsible for the health and well-being of those who attack you.**

... *let people pull him down, no matter how close they are to him.*

Our path forward

In **Step 5**, we learned strategies to handle conflict better with maturity in mind.

In **Step 6**, we'll learn new ways to view and resist temptations.

RESIST TEMPTATIONS

I generally avoid temptation unless I can't resist it.
~ Mae West

You'll want to slow down at this intersection.

S tep 6 wasn't supposed to be in this book. I shared the original nine steps with my good friend Bob, a police officer, who recognized the deficiency right away.

"Steve, those nine steps are great," he said, "but you are missing a really important piece about human nature."

"Really?"

Bob nodded. "Most people can't resist temptations, no matter how well-intentioned they are."

A light went off in my head. I was one of those people.

Each step in this book is important because omitting any of them will impair your ability to restart your best life. But Step 6 is critical. If you don't resist temptations, you *will* ruin the quality of your life.

Let's face it, we're all tempted at various times in our lives. We get bored and it's often much easier to do the wrong thing than it is to do the right thing. We need to control the mischievous devil-on-our-shoulder.

Whether it's sex, food, computers, sugar, greed, anger, laziness, or addictions like liquor and drugs, we all have weaknesses. We can't pretend otherwise. We have to face temptations, outlast the devil, outwit ourselves, and out-pedal our urges to take the easy way.

The downfalls of President Bill Clinton, movie mogul Harvey Weinstein, and television personality Bill Cosby are proof positive. All three succumbed to sexual indiscretions or crimes. Obviously, temptation is not exclusive to the rich and famous; it's part of all of us.

My friend Bob went on to relate how two fellow police officers, each of (otherwise) good character and with bright futures, had an affair. They were publicly humiliated and lost their jobs and families. All because they didn't fight temptation.

Temptations lure us to something that feels good in the moment. However, the good feelings don't last. Very quickly, the results of our temptation-tainted actions set us on a toxic path, one that derails our best selves. We harm others. We lose our way. Success is more difficult to achieve.

When we think it through, resisting makes sense. Following through and actually resisting is the hard part.

To be successful, we can refuse temptations completely or find ways to mollify our urges. Reading into the examples above, human nature allows denial in theory only. In practice, we need to mitigate our self-destructive urges by finding character-building replacement activities.

The successful people I know fill their time with activities that either build their physical stamina as in Step 4, or they find ways to help others. Whether you work at a soup kitchen like my friend Steve or volunteer for a library reading program, productive activities like these help others and help keep you away from temptations.

Rather than relying on resistance or denial to keep the devil at arm's length, you can and should:

- Question your urges to do the wrong thing. Figure out what is at the root of those temptations. Know the times when your urges present themselves. Fill that time with character-building activities.

- Incentivize replacement activities by enhancing their value. If you find yourself too interested in surfing the web at night or staying too long on the computer (inviting problems), perhaps you could phone a family member, read a good book, or take a walk. Find an unmet need in your community. Help out.

- Consider re-igniting a fun hobby to fill your time. Perhaps you collected stamps or cards as a kid. That's a great place to start.

- Refresh your goals and remind yourself of the consequences of falling into temptation. Ask yourself questions like:

  - *Is today the day I want to ruin my life?*

- *Is this the day I enter the slippery slope that negatively changes my life?*

- *What will my family and friends think of me if this activity becomes known?*

My friend Stuart has the heart of a champion and the pride of a lion. No one is more disciplined. At age seventy-one, Stuart was the New England Xterra Champion—swimming, mountain biking, and mountain running—for eight years in a row. But that wasn't always the case.

Thirty years before his Xterra success, Stuart smoked a pack a day of Marlboro cigarettes. He wasn't the poster boy for resisting anything. When he stopped smoking, he vowed to return his health to top status. And he did it! He called it Tamping Down the Beast.

Stuart's Story

As a child I was husky, a five-letter euphemism for the three letters we all hate: F-A-T. Thanks to the U.S. Army and ten months in Vietnam, I lost my huskiness, but I picked up a few dirty habits, among them smoking. That habit lasted about twenty years.

A little over thirty years ago, I quit smoking and vowed to keep the weight off. I bought a used, multi-geared Fuji road bike. For the next six months, I rode 100-150 miles each week. I enjoyed riding and my excess weight peeled off, but it was hard work.

I rode the Fuji into the ground and learned it would cost more to repair than to buy a new bike. With that incentive, I bought a high-end racing bike and continued to ride. To give my quads a break and add some diversity to my exercise, I started running, too.

At my job with a travel tour operator, I struck up a conversation about off-work activities with our marketing director, Roberta. I told her about my biking and running. She asked if I swam.

"I did when I was younger," I admitted.

"Have you ever thought about doing triathlons?" she asked.

Puzzled, I could only respond, "What's a triathlon?"

With that one question, Roberta opened a world I had never before experienced. I discovered an athlete inside me who loved the competitive excitement of racing. My first race was in 1981 in Dedham, Massachusetts. I finished in first place and was hooked.

I wanted to improve my race times and learn any new skill that would advance me in triathlons. Focusing on food choices, exercise, and endurance, I developed a different self-image. I was no longer the husky boy. I was a triathlete. That new identity keeps the devil of temptation at bay.

I met Steve after I had been competing for over twenty years. Steve was, shall we say, husky and an avid mountain biker, but a neophyte to triathlons. We rode often and I shared my love of triathlons.

I became his role model for exercise. Steve had never seen anyone maintain physical conditioning into their sixties. After a year of riding together, I asked him to do a brick with me.

"What's a brick?" Steve asked.

"A brick," I explained, "is a term triathletes use to describe multiple training sessions in a row—without stopping to rest in between."

Steve was astounded. He thought if you rode for an hour or swam a half-mile, you were done. You needn't do anything else. I was replacing his frame for exercise—and he caught on.

We trained together for the next triathlon. Soon, he participated in the New Jersey Devil Triathlon with me. (Curious title, isn't it, given the subject matter of Step 6?) Steve came in last, and he will tell you that he didn't do well.

But he did it!

When Steve expressed frustration with his weight, his diet, and training for the swim, the coach in me surfaced. To my surprise, I had lots to share about eating healthy and how to race. By this time, I had done hundreds of triathlons and could give great tips. So many, in fact, I'm compiling them into a book: *100 Tips for Your Best Triathlon*.

Now, at seventy-one, I can still do a one-mile swim, followed by a twelve-mile mountain bike ride, and a four-mile run in less than four hours.

As earnest as I am about encouraging triathletes and being a role model, I want Steve and others to know that under the surface, is a martini-swilling, chain-smoking fat man. That devil pesters me now just as he did thirty years ago. I fear the lazy guy in me might return. I continue my struggle. Fear motivates me.

Stuart has kept his pesky devil at bay, yet I find it ironic that one of the most fearless people I've ever met uses fear to hold off his personal temptation. But it's hard to argue with great results! Clearly Stuart replaced his urges with creative challenges, what some might call a replacement addiction—an addiction with far better consequences.

My friend Claudinhea shared with me her take on resisting: "If there is ever a question about whether I should or shouldn't, I ask myself, 'Is it a win-win? Does anyone benefit other than me?' If the answers are *no*, my internal guide is pointing out a much better direction."

The recurring theme of all my friends' stories is: Stay busy to fight boredom. Dave D. helped others. Stuart became a triathlon champion. Luis ran marathons, using meditation that added value to his family life. I do public service announcements and interviews. None of us has time left for temptations.

Filling gaps of bored time with activities that benefit yourself and others stabilizes and rounds out your life.

Keep yourself busy. Steel yourself, by any and all means, to deny the easy. Lean toward the hard. The difficult.

Like my wonderful, marathon-crazy friend Luis, we must find ways to tolerate pain. When we recognize our weaknesses, we can build an approach that will douse the fires of unproductive desire.

In closing this section, I'd like to share a warning captured in the entertaining twist of this fable: If you succumb to temptations and selfish behavior, you might end up like the two brothers in this story.

The Mensch

Two wealthy Jewish brothers, the epitome of selfishness and boorish behavior, offended everyone in their community. They insulted people, accusing their children of being lazy and wives useless. The brothers derided their own family members. They cheated on their wives and, of course, lied about it.

Those two men gave stingy and rotten a whole new meaning.

When the synagogue building committee sought funding for a renovation and expansion, the two brothers couldn't be bothered.

It so happened that just as a new rabbi replaced the retiring rabbi, one of the wealthy brothers died. The surviving brother went to see the new rabbi and asked him to give the eulogy at the funeral.

"And," he wheedled, "if you will praise my brother, say he was a *mensch*, (a wonderful, kind, giving person), I will underwrite the entire cost of the synagogue renovations."

He promptly produced a check and waved it temptingly under the rabbi's nose.

The rabbi, who had been briefed by the outgoing rabbi about the two brothers, was beside himself. He knew how important this renovation was, but he also was sworn to high standards, to uphold truth.

"I … I'll sleep on it and give you my decision in the morning," he said.

The next day, the rabbi met with the surviving brother. He agreed to give the eulogy—and accepted the check.

At the funeral that afternoon, the rabbi—to the shock and horror of the living brother—offered the eulogy and proceeded to tell the congregation that the deceased had been an awful person … had abused his children in every way … had cheated on his wife … had left much of his wealth to his girlfriend … had swindled his business associates and screwed his friends.

Just as the livid surviving brother started to jump to his feet in protest, the rabbi ended with,

"—but, compared to his brother, **he was a real** *mensch*!"

SUMMARY

We learned that we all have temptations that must be tamed. Even those who deal well with temptations fight, and even fear, their devils. We need to recognize our urges and redirect the stimulation with activities with better outcomes.

Action Steps to Resist Temptations

1. Recognize your temptations. Accept that we all have a devil to resist.

2. Add replacement activities to answer urges in productive ways.

3. Picture yourself on the front page of your local newspaper doing what is tempting you.

4. Think of someone you admire. Ask yourself, "What would she think of me?"

5. Fight boredom. Volunteer and involve yourself in a higher cause.

6. Always leave things better than you find them. Don't just walk past or walk away.

7. Repeat this mantra: My demons don't control me.

8. Raise your standards. Ask and expect better of yourself. Be better than you were yesterday.

A genius probably wouldn't

... *keep friends who aren't growing with him, or who aren't up to his speed.*

... *create options that set him up for failure.*

... *be idle for extended amounts of time. The devil makes work for idle hands.*

Our path forward

In Step 6, we learned new ways to view and resist temptations in life.

In Step 7, we'll focus on building *karma*.

BUILD KARMA

When you have a child, it changes your world view. Overnight, it becomes important that the world succeed! ~ Susan DeBalsi

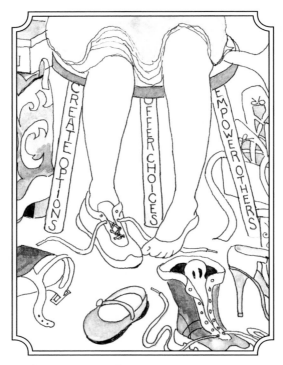

Create options, offer choices, empower others

When we want the world to succeed, we practice *karma*; we act with deep concern for others. You notice people with *karma*. They glow, or at least I think they do. People, after all, are walking reflections of their pasts, and karma is their energy projecting into the future.

As I began writing this step, I realized my friend Paul, a ceiling tile contractor, is a shining example of how you can add *karma* to your life. The people he helped in the following story were also great *karma* producers.

I went to Paul for a favor. "Hey, Paul, do you have a moment for me to ask something of you?" I thought I framed it cleverly as I continued.

"Don't worry. It's not going to cost you too much."

No slouch at framing either, Paul responded predictably with an eye roll. "Oh, crap, what are you up to now?"

I laughed. "Really, it's something small."

"Yeah, yeah," he retorted, "spit it out!"

So I told him about three delightful friends of mine, The Memory Ladies, who had each, unfortunately, lost a child. They were heroically trying to survive by starting The Memory Room, a nonprofit dedicated to helping others who experienced similar events. The ladies came to me for tiles to draw images on for their office ceiling, a truly unique idea.

"So, I wonder, Paul, if you could sell the ladies some tiles at your wholesale cost. That would give them a real discount—"

"No!" Paul interrupted.

Not wanting to offend, and being empathetic to the difficulty of running a small business, I back-pedaled right away. "No problem, Paul. It's a tough economy out there and—"

He jumped in again. "I know those ladies and it breaks my heart to think of what they've been through. No discount. I'll give them the tiles for free."

Before I could register my surprise, Paul added, "To get good results, though, they need to use these special tiles I have in stock, which will be easiest to draw on."

"Wow, Paul. This is generous of you. Thanks!"

Paul showed me the shipment, new 2x2' tiles. They would look great for the portraits and art envisioned by The Memory Ladies.

Unfortunately, when I arrived at the Memory Room, I saw their ceiling tile grid layout was for 2x4' tiles, and not the size Paul offered.

I returned to his office.

"Paul, the tiles won't work. The suite would need small cross tees to break up each tile bay for the newer, smaller 2x2' ceiling tiles." I knew the application, with the tiles and labor, would cost over $ 1,000, much more expensive than either of us expected.

"Your offer of free tiles was gracious and generous, Paul, but I can't ask you to contribute what it would take to convert their ceiling grid."

The office was silent for a long minute, until Paul barked at me in a terse voice. "Steve, I'm trying to get to heaven. Let me do this!"

My grin stretched ear-to-ear.

What a guy. I think Paul will get to heaven! His *karma* is strong.

Here's another *karma*-producing story about my stepson, Dave, who attended Wade Boggs's minor league baseball tribute game at McCoy Stadium in Pawtucket, Rhode Island, several years back.

Dave and his friend Nick hoped to be among the first five thousand fans to arrive at the stadium in order to receive a coveted bobble-head statue commemorating Boggs's hard-won eighteen-year, twelve all-star-seasons career. But they arrived late to the park, paid $6 for their tickets, and ended up as far in right field as being tardy can get you.

As Dave and Nick sought the perfect place to watch the game, they spied two unoccupied stools at a four-seat table overlooking the field at the foul pole. Two fifty-something business types welcomed them at the table.

In the third inning, Nick reached his six-foot frame over the outstretched arms of several kids to catch a foul ball, which he promptly stashed in his pocket for his collection. The youngsters, whom he had cleanly outreached, clung to the foul-pole rail and stared at every pitch, waiting for the next opportunity.

One much smaller boy hung back, waiting for his chance, hoping that by some stroke of luck, the ball might careen off the others in their nervous excitement to catch it.

The older gentlemen next to Dave and Nick struck up casual conversation to reminisce about Boggs's eleven great years with the Red Sox. Dave remembered seeing the colorful Boggs at a game with his dad fifteen years earlier when he was a scrawny twelve-year-old. He remembered how his dad had caught a foul fly ball off of Jody Reed's bat. (Jody was a better-than-average second baseman who played well for the Sox in 1987-1992.)

Dave's dad had reached for the ball, snatching it in an acrobatic move, but some guy in a plaid shirt grabbed his arm and tried to yank the ball from his grasp.

Remembering it as clearly as if it had happened yesterday, Dave told his tablemates, "Dad threw the hardest elbow I'd ever seen thrown, and the plaid-shirt guy slumped to his chair. Dad grabbed that ball for me."

As it turned out, the seats Dave and Nick had found really were the perfect spot for foul balls, even if they had come too late for the bobble-head statues. By the fourth inning a second foul ball reached their spot and this time twenty-seven-year-old Dave, with his manly 6'2" frame, reached out and plucked the ball from the outstretched arms of the boys. It was a great catch, TV shot for sure.

When he sat back down, one of the two older fellows at his table nudged Dave and asked unexpectedly, "What would it take to get you to give the little guy over there your ball?"

Dave's recent memory tugged at him. His face contorted as his eyes met those of the older gentleman. With a nod and a sigh, he walked over and gave his ball to the scrawny boy at the back of the group.

The youngster's face lit up. He clung to the ball as if it were a life-line, showing it off to his friends with a firm, two-fisted grip. No one was taking that ball from him!

Dave sat taller in his seat.

The older gentleman, one of the lucky five thousand to receive the Boggs's bobble-head, pushed the statue across the table to Dave. "Thanks, kid. That was nice of ya."

An inning later, the second gentleman asked Dave, in a voice just loud enough for Nick to hear, "What'll it take to get your buddy to fork over that other ball to those kids?"

Half-dejectedly and half-disgustedly, Nick rolled his eyes, sighed heavily, and walked over to the kids at the foul pole. He reluctantly gave his ball to a delighted youngster. Wearing a smirk, he walked back to the table. Without saying a word, the gentleman dutifully placed his bobble-head in Nick's outstretched hands.

Dave's dad, if he could have seen him, would have beamed with pride over his son and Nick who, without an elbow thrown, made their own all-star moves.

No doubt in fifteen years, on a sunny day at McCoy or some other stadium honoring another deserving sports legend, there will be two young adults, a new group of scrawny young kids with eager hands, and two older gentlemen named Dave and Nick. They'll know exactly what to do.

The kind of grace-producing energy—shared by Paul and The Memory Ladies, by Dave and Nick, and the two older gentlemen—starts with concern for others. Empathy and volunteering builds your *karma*.

SUMMARY

Creating and teaching *karma* through selfless acts is important.

Action Steps to Build *Karma*

1. Volunteer wherever you see a need. Be generous with your time. Great surprise endings will come your way.

2. Build a habit of saying thank you, at least three times each day, to those who help you or have helped you in the past.

3. The environment matters. Fix some part of it every day. Pick up litter. Recycle. Leave things better than you find them.

4. Spend time advising, mentoring, or helping those in need of guidance.

5. Do something nice for someone who could never repay you.

6. Pick a different person to do something nice for every week. If someone you know is having a tough time, call them to see how they are doing, or invite them out.

A genius probably wouldn't...

    ... *berate others.*

      → *Genius thinking: Bishop Desmond Tutu famously said, "If I diminish you, I diminish myself." Speaking poorly about others is not good for your* karma.

    ... *be a cynic.*

      → *Genius thinking: Cynics can't make good* karma *happen.*

Our path forward

~~~~~~

In Step 7, we learned the importance of *karma* and how to build it.

In Step 8, we'll focus on how you can develop your best future by Finding Your Fit.

FIND YOUR FIT

You can't put a square peg in a round hole.
~ Sydney Smith

*There is nothing so fulfilling in life as finding what
one is meant to do, and doing it.*

When my twin teenage grandchildren, Cam and Chloe, started thinking about careers, I wanted to help them make choices that would ensure their success, happiness, and fulfillment. I didn't want them to repeat my mistakes. I wished I could give simple guidance: "You guys are like young thoroughbreds in a horse race. Break out of the gate fast, run hard to the bend, stay off the rails, and finish strong. You'll win and be happy forever."

Whether you are a COVID-19 casualty, fresh out of college, or graduating from high school like Cam and Chloe, guidance for careers or life isn't that simple. Neither is an easily-won race. In fact, a race frame doesn't fit the situation at all. A puzzle is a more useful analogy to help you understand how to find your fit.

Think about the process of building a puzzle. It's mostly trial and error. Having someone over your shoulder telling you to try this piece, or that piece, doesn't work. You have to do it yourself, by methodically moving the pieces around to find their proper places.

The process of finding *your* place is the same kind of trial and error process. The information you gather from education, former jobs, part-time jobs, and internships become pieces of your puzzle. Eventually the pieces interlock and you begin to see your fit.

My grandchildren's task (and your task) is to try lots of new things, test and evaluate different jobs, different industries, and different lifestyles until you feel yourself getting closer to your potential. It takes time, so be patient.

Sometimes you'll get helpful advice from friends or family, but no amount of advice can take the place of the process of testing and re-evaluating in the real world. Finding your fit gets easier after you've been knocked around a bit.

As your puzzle comes together, you will understand more of the big picture, a complex task. It's comforting to know that this period of growth—finding yourself and integrating with the larger world—parallels other generations. My grandchildren's generation now has an added challenge.

COVID-19 OR SUPERBUG 2050

Whether it's this novel coronavirus or another superbug in 2050, the journey of discovery will be complex, —but not necessarily more difficult. Here's why: Disruption creates opportunity. The greater the disruption, the greater the opportunities.

Before this disruption of global isolation and stalled economies, old patterns and tightly-controlled systems impeded new entrants to the working world. Now, due to seismic shifts in work patterns, disrupted systems, and unemployment exacerbated by safety concerns of COVID-19, the entire idea of career may become obsolete.

In an economy no one envisioned, there are no experts but plenty of opportunities to become one. Go-getters who flexibly re-envision themselves to catch new opportunities will succeed.

This next generation might call themselves the Salamander Generation, as they constantly adapt to fit in a fast-changing world. Successful new job entrants will adapt their interests, talents, and personalities into this COVID-19 puzzle and make room for future, unknown puzzles, too.

History is filled with courageous people facing significant tumults: the Great Depression, World Wars I and II, Vietnam, 9/11, the SARS and Ebola epidemics. We, too, will stretch, sacrifice, and overcome this massive pandemic. Charles Beard, a famous historian, sets an instructive, universal tone for assessing human history in this great, four-line verse:

Whom the Gods wish to destroy, they first drive mad with power.

The mills of God grind slowly, but exceedingly small.

The bee robs the flower it fertilizes.

Only when it is truly dark, can one see all the stars.

Beard's last line provides us the hope we need. We are in a situation whose severity sharpens our focus on what is important and stimulates our direction and urgency.

Because of the speed of change facing us, our futures depend more than ever on wherewithal, flexibility, and ingenuity. Those who draw upon these three characteristics will be able to successfully integrate into an increasingly difficult and unpredictable environment.

Scott's Story

My friend Scott does what he loves and it shows. He's sharp-witted, physical, brainy, curious and playful, a guy who loves a challenge. He's also not afraid to speak his mind. If you ask Scott a question while he's trying to figure something out, he'll snap back, "Not now!"

His characteristics mesh well with the career he chose: an HVAC (heating, ventilation, and air conditioning) mechanic.

When I first met Scott, his helper was complaining about him. I told his helper that Scott was just being cantankerous. Scott overheard me, and gave a semi-serious retort.

"Don't call me that!"

The truth is he didn't know what the word meant.

That night Scott, ever the researcher, looked up cantankerous. When he found synonyms like argumentative, quick-tempered, crabby, and grumpy, Scott admitted, "Yep. That's me."

Scott lives for bad winters, faulty heating systems, and air conditioning meltdowns in 100-degree heat. Recently he came to fix our gas heating system.

With a Sherlock Holmes mindset and a come-Watson-the-game-is-afoot attitude, Scott quickly assimilated the clues he needed to find the system fault. He deduced that the gas flame sensor, with its milliamp conductor, wasn't reading the flame in the burner.

With emery cloth from his truck, he cleared the excessive coking on the contact, re-inserted the part, and *WHAM-O!* Back in business. As the system fired up, Scott brimmed with satisfaction. Problem diagnosed; problem fixed. In *ten minutes*. No parts replaced, time only. That's a cheap repair, so I was thrilled.

Out of curiosity, I asked, "Why do you enjoy this HVAC stuff so much? And what keeps you interested in it?"

Scott leaned against his truck. "I love problem-solving and the work is interesting. It's different at each job and with each new system." Grinning, he added, "No piece of metal is going to out-think me! I ain't gonna get beat by an inanimate object."

With his great attitude, job fit, and mindset, you can easily see why Scott is successful. His company recognizes the value he brings to their customers. They support him. And sustainability as an HVAC technician is strong. There will always be service work for good technicians in the HVAC field.

Whether you own a roofing company or a restaurant, are rebuilding your landscaping or salon businesses, post-COVID-19 success stories will depend on better fundamentals, better cash flow, and tighter operations from A-Z. (Government stimulus packages will disappear, perhaps never to be seen again.)

There's never a better time to follow Scott's example and find your best fit in the workforce. The following six dimensions will help you identify your skills, recognize your passions, consider your ingenuity, search out sustainability, understand your values, and grow your income.

As you strive to reach your highest potential, start here:

1. Inherent Strengths

Identify what you are naturally good at. Be flexible, even if the job isn't what you think you'll do for the long-term.

Look wider and broader than those around you. In the post-COVID-19 era, with millions unemployed, you will need to break from your previous ideas of job, career, and lifestyle to find that new fit.

Like each of us, companies will struggle for their own *raison d'être*— reason to exist. Regardless of the environment or the form employment takes, finding your fit will always make your future better.

Catalogue the things you've already tried with good results. Find new ideas that require you to take risks and open your mind to new possibilities. Chicago Tribune writer Mary Schmich said, "Do something every day that scares you." Seek out the unfamiliar and awkward.

My unfamiliar and awkward storytelling experience opened the door to a new life of teaching and self-improvement. Boris Pasternak, the famous Soviet poet and author of *Doctor Zhivago*, said "When a great moment knocks on the door of your life, it is often no louder than the beating of your heart, and it is very easy to miss it." Take his lesson to heart.

Listen to your intuition. Notice your feelings when you do new things. Make a list of things that make you curious and uncomfortable. Those are places to explore.

2. Passions

Identify what you love to do.

Write down the five or six things you love to do most. Is it listening to music? Playing a sport? Researching genealogy? What about photography? Farming? Cooking? History? Travel? Video games? Writing? Reading? Software? Healthy eating and nutrition? What are the things you would do if you weren't getting paid?

My friend Len loves photography. Len took the picture to the left. He got a part-time job taking Boston Celtics game day pictures. He couldn't survive on that income alone, but he loved the work and parlayed his love for photography into a healthy "birding" hobby that led to more opportunities.

Brainstorm interesting occupations or vocations that could utilize several of your talents and passions. Scott likes to research and loves to solve puzzles. Those skills fit nicely into his repair work.

If you like history and travel, a career as tour guide seems a natural fit. If you like music and carpentry, consider guitar design and repair. Perhaps your love of video games and architecture equates to video game design for you. Or you might combine a love of sports with your interest in healthy eating and become an endurance athletic coach.

Perhaps you enjoy writing and helping people learn. You could write business plans, language skill books, or even how-to books. If you see yourself as a protector, explore security, detective, or police work. Or maybe your love of farming could make you a coordinator for CSA shares and farmers markets?

If you are passionate about improving our environment, home goods and transportation with solar-powered innovations like electric cars, lighting, and appliances are great places to focus and explore to find your fit.

Whether it's exercise like yoga, swimming, soccer, basketball, baseball, mountain biking, or cricket, instruction and coaching are always in need. Systems repair like Scott's work in HVAC opens up another world of opportunity for those who are not only good with their hands, but also sharp in diagnostics.

The possibilities are endless as you examine ways your interests and skills can equate to a fulfilling career.

3. Market Needs

Identify deficiencies of the world-at-large.

Do you see a hole you can fill in the market? Do you have innovative ideas others have missed? Do you envision a job or business to fulfill an upsurge in demand?

With existing systems upside down, believe it or not, the world has more needs and unique opportunities than ever before. Ross Perot, 1992 presidential candidate and Texas billionaire, built his fortune on the credo: *Find an unmet need and fill it.*

Look to find those unique opportunities and create new ones through innovation. Consider how you might take existing resources and re-apply them to new problems.

In response to the scarcity of N95 masks during the novel coronavirus pandemic, individuals made their own masks with unique combinations of elastics, plastic, unused fabrics, and buttons—a great example of innovation and ingenuity.

Innovation will reign supreme as the Salamander Generation steps into the marketplace with fresh concepts and energy.

Refer back to the occupations brain-stormed above and consider how every one of them has global application to fulfill the needs of millions. There is demand even as that demand morphs to take on new shapes and needs.

4. Job Sustainability

For all who have traveled the bumpy road of COVID-19, sustainability is key. As you assess potential employers, take a hard look at benefit packages.

Medical, educational, and retirement benefits are significant factors in your decision—but be wary of over-weighing these factors. COVID-19 destroyed many companies. Good careers and great benefit packages went right out the window.

Whether working for others or yourself, give some thought to the business model that will provide your livelihood. To protect your financial future, think about whether the business you are joining is sustainable. Does the company have recurring and residual income streams? Does their business model consistently create value for its clients?

As you explore sustainability, forget for a moment what the job means to you and focus on the important question of how the business model creates value for its clients. If that isn't a paramount concern for the business you are joining, you'll revisit unemployment quickly.

As you check out new career and job possibilities, consider the Japanese concept of *Ikigai* (pronounced eye-ka-guy), which roughly translates to "a reason for being." In their book *Ikigai*, Hector Garcia and Francesc Miralles share four dimensions that lock together when we find our *Ikigai*.

5. Culture

As you look for your best fit, don't minimize the importance of work-place culture—the environment, customs, and conventions of the company you are considering.

Questions like these will help you assess culture:

- Are there work-from-home options?

- Does the company believe in promoting from within? Or does the company prefer to outsource and bring in outside talent?

- Can the business accommodate paternity leave along with maternity leave?

- Is the workplace a lone-wolf operation? Or is it team-focused?

- Does it create a learning environment? Or is it a production-only shop?

- Does the business recycle? Is it environmentally aware?

Next, quiz yourself, a process to shed light on areas of importance you might not know or otherwise consider.

- Are creativity and learning at work important to me?

- Is work merely a requirement for survival? Or do I need my job to fulfill me?

- Do I need a nurturing workplace?

- Am I a self-starter who thrives on minimal supervision?

To answer these questions and identify your values, remove yourself from time-sucks like Twitter and Facebook. Although useful social platforms, they come at a high cost to the quiet time necessary for the important job of introspection.

6. Income

Recognize that getting paid well is an integral part of finding your fit. Demand good pay. Of course, good pay and reasonable income are subjective assessments. It may take a while to land on your feet. Consider introductory pay offers to be a starting point. Take what you can get and build from there.

Poet/musician Joshua Kadison sings, "Every man sells a bit of his soul to bring his family home some gold."

As you settle into your next phase, it may not be a dream job or dream setting, but remember: Your goal is a smooth fit between work, home life, and values. You'll get there with a dedicated one-step-at-a-time approach and the same holds true for earnings. They will fluctuate and grow with you as you gain experience and skills and will continue to offer more value.

For those in third and fourth career phases, compensation may not be as strong a determinant, but finding meaningful work and adequate compensation is still important. Your goal might be to simply find sustainable support that fulfills you.

Even in observing these six dimensions, it's likely you'll run into snags. Obstacles confront all of us at one time or another. Elbow your way through them, climb over them, skirt them … do what you must to keep your eye on your goal: the best job or career fit you can manage.

As I broke the curse of my personal background, I cobbled together my own fulfilling livelihood. Using the ideas above, I now co-manage a small family real estate development and management business with my two sons. This provides our regular income along with long-term, recurring, residual income. We accrue wealth in the form of property appreciation and debt reduction through principal payments.

I also teach communication and business courses. With my sons, I own and co-manage a roofing company, which provides regular earnings.

By combining my three part-time jobs, I'm able to create a solid income, control how my home life fits with my work life, and protect my personal, discretionary time for writing and exercising. This hybrid conception of *Ikigai* works well for me.

Ikigai is a tall order. To get the best result, try to incorporate as many of these dimensions in your livelihood and employment choices as possible.

～～～～～ SUMMARY ～～～～～

Finding your fit helps you realize your highest potential. You need to take stock of your talents and characteristics and find the best match in a work environment. When your values, passions, and competencies mesh with your job, fit with your home life, and are sustainable, you will find a place to shine.

Action Steps to Find Your Fit

1. Make a list of things you are good at.

2. Make a list of things you enjoy doing—even if you didn't get paid.

3. Merge the lists of what you love and what you are good at to brainstorm job ideas.

4. Explore new ideas, to use your creative instincts—do things that make you smile.

5. Meditate to gain mindfulness and awareness of who you are.

6. Take classes on things that interest you or pique your curiosity: cooking, yoga, knitting, writing, farming, etc.

7. Consider how your job impacts your home life (enhance vs. harm).

8. Give a nod to how your work can create sustainability in your future.

A genius probably wouldn't...

... take a job with values that don't match hers.

... stay in a job where the people and culture aren't a fit.

... take a job she doesn't like, unless she must for survival.

... listen to a back-seat driver.

... aspire to a job that doesn't pay well.

Our path forward

In Step 8, we focused on ways to find a solid fit between our values and strengths, our work choices and the workplace environment, to help make our future better.

In Step 9, we'll focus on balancing and energizing our lives with fun.

BALANCE YOUR
LIFE WITH FUN

Into the earth I go

On the Oak leaf I stand

I ride on a filly that's never been foaled

And I carry the dead in my hand.

~ Anonymous Storytelling Introduction

Make everyday amazing with fun!

N ot too high. Not too low. Just right.

To stay balanced in the middle, you need to open the door and let your inner child come out to play. Having fun is as important as working hard.

Your inner child wants go to the park, share a story, see a play, or go for a swim. The adult in you too often says, "No. I need to work."

Your inner child understands what your adult side doesn't: Fun nurtures you and provides positive energy to fuel your ability to live a more exciting and rewarding life—something we all want.

How much better is it to listen to your inner child!

I find deep pleasure in bike riding, doing yoga, sharing stories, and being open to new experiences. With that in mind, I make sure to include at least one of these delightful activities every day to stay balanced.

The good news? This habit energizes me so that I work smarter and get my work done more easily.

The bad news? Fun, itself, takes work. You must be disciplined in order to open, restore, and maintain space in your life for it. It seems confusing, like a catch-22 scenario, but it's not.

Restoring the space for fun begins with saying a resounding "No!" to more responsibilities. No, I can't babysit your dog. No, I don't want to go for coffee. No, I don't want to go to the party.

When I say, "yes" to those requests, I lose the extra time that could be reserved for or converted to entertainment, sports, and hobbies— whatever delights the soul.

You can unravel that damned-if-you-do-and-damned-if-you-don't conundrum by reframing your understanding of how fun impacts your ability to work.

Too often, we don't feel good about the work we do. We don't keep a positive mindset, letting our jobs create too much stress. When our workload wears at us, it makes us dull and one-dimensional. It's true. People who work too much are boring.

High workloads can overwhelm anyone. We don't make our best choices when we are tired and engulfed. We must work less and work smarter to make better choices. Taking daily doses of fun helps Break the Curse to build a great life.

By engaging in pleasurable activities that meet those needs, you increase your joy.

Pleasurable activities are multi-faceted. They might relax, invigorate, challenge, calm, delight, amuse, enthuse, teach, satisfy …. Which do you need in your life to balance your load, your input, your emotional or physical or spiritual side?

Hopefully, you are grinning and sighing with a thank-God breath of relief, because you need a break!

And, perhaps, permission to play.

As a child, I lived for fun; it was my highest purpose and I couldn't get enough of it. I remember fighting to keep work out of my life. The opposite shouldn't be true just because we get older.

In case you aren't convinced, think for a minute about doing the opposite of having more fun. Let's eliminate fun from our lives. How might you do that?

To start, let's make fun illegal. We'll give small fines for smiles and bigger fines for laughing. A belly laugh will get you jail time. Next we'll stack as many responsibilities as possible onto your shoulders: holding multiple jobs, caregiving for an infirm parent, raising kids, doing house repairs, dealing with money woes. And we'll add a giant spoonful of guilt for not reaching your potential.

If you recognize parts and pieces of your current situation in this "fun" exercise, injecting real fun activities in your life will make sense for you.

You might think that you don't have time for frivolity. You might even think that I'm off the rails now. If I am, that's where you need to go, too, because without fun the rails are in the wrong place in your life. Fun has to be a track we take purposefully and often.

Joy and creativity won't appear when your head is buried in work. You won't find it by constantly posting to social media.

Playfulness begins by reviving your inner spirit. You'll see and feel the difference. You might even reach a level of "nauseatingly bubbly."

When I first entered triathlons, I was elated even when I came in last. Others who finished ahead of me, groused at their placements if their run time wasn't good. They were aggravated if their swim time was too long. I was just happy to be present and engaged in such a challenging and uplifting activity. I relished in the joy of being able to swim, bike, and run. The same joy held steady and fortified me as I recovered from cancer.

That same positive attitude—achieved through balance, helped me become a successful contractor, real estate manager, professor, and author. Thinking negatively would have closed off my potential.

As you work through your tough times, being positive and finding the rainbow in the clouds isn't easy, but it's there, and anyone can do it.

You don't need rose-colored, rainbow-chasing glasses. You need to believe in yourself, learn from your failures, and balance your life with doses of fun—the prescription that clarifies your perception and enables you to look for the positive in everything you do.

Several years ago when I was teaching an effective listening course, a particular student (who had been one of the Vietnamese boat children in the Saigon flotilla of 1975) made an indelible mark on the class and on me.

As we explored the elements of listening—from the physical (the role of the cochlea) to the spiritual (the Chinese symbol for listening is also the symbol for heart), I asked each student to share a personal definition of listening.

Most students struggled. Liem Le, who didn't usually say much, nailed it. He gave us the best explanation I had ever heard.

Liem's parents—officers in the South Vietnamese Army when Saigon fell to the North Vietnamese in 1975—knew their fate and made the unthinkable and courageous decision to give up their children for a new life of hope. Even without the certainty of a sure result. How hard it must have been for them!

At the tender ages of six and two, Liem and his little sister were placed on boats to travel from Vietnam to England to Australia to the United States.

Liem told our class his harrowing story of endurance, how he protected his sister through their dangerous journey. His skill for survival at such a young age? He listened intently in order to discern what was happening around him. Listening—being able to truly *hear*, meant that he first had to "liberate himself from his own thinking."

Liberate himself from his own thinking.

I was stunned. I knew immediately that Liem Le had taught us the true meaning of listening: to ***liberate yourself from your own thinking***.

This was brilliant. This was magic. What an absolutely clear and invincible definition Liem gave!

As the teacher taught by the student, I've used Liem's definition to bolster my own listening skills ever since. In my volunteer work as a TV host interviewing hundreds of people for a local cable station, I use his magical definition as my mantra. Before each interview, I repeat the phrase, *Liberate yourself from your own thinking,* which repositions me to engage people with *karma* and to truly get to know them. I am honored to have had Liem Le as my teacher.

Most importantly, liberating myself from my own thinking—in this case, that work is all-important—frees me for reflective listening. It allows me to listen to my inner child and make time for fun. For passion. For joy.

~~~~~~~~~

More time needs to be spent in our carefree-child place. By breaking free of the adult expectations we place on ourselves, we find much-needed spontaneous and raw enjoyment. Playtime is just as important for adults. It's not that work isn't important, or that we should avoid work. It is vital that we balance play and work to create our best life.

Focus on freeing the child within you.

Find people who make you laugh.

Develop and engage in activities that enthrall and energize you.

When nature presents a rainbow, pause and take it in. Too often people don't stop to smell the roses. As trite as the saying is, it's totally true.

My son Phil has a saying: *We're here for a good time, not a long time.* While I wouldn't give that tidbit as stand-alone guidance, I do believe we need to focus more on making the present a good time.

We need to create memorable moments with families and friends. Sometimes, we need to break away from over-stimulation, sit by a river, reflect … and let the magic of life come to us in a tranquil space.

~~~~~

Be mindful that technology is taking away the deep, quiet space people need to listen and grow. Too much time is spent on computers and cellphones, on Twitter, Facebook, Instagram, Snapchat, and all of the social media platforms. Let's change that for everyone's benefit.

SUMMARY

Build fun into your life. Fun invigorates us, stabilizes us, balances our equilibrium—and revitalizes our energy through childlike joy. When we reconnect to intense joy, our imaginations steer our lives in positive ways.

Don't let the clouds take away your sunshine, let sunshine take you out of the clouds.

Action Steps to Balance Your Life with Fun

1. Do creative, joy-filled activities.

2. Laugh often. Laugh like it's the last time you'll get a chance to laugh.

3. See what a child sees and tell that curmudgeon to stay home.

4. Spend time with family doing childlike things.

5. Keep your curiosity alive. It frees you from sheltering inside of yourself and keeps you interested in the world. Ask: "why," "why," and "why" again to make sure you have good reasons for saying, "yes" when you should say "no."

6. Make time to create and tell your own imaginative stories with everyone.

7. Try carefully walking backwards ten steps each day. Use the activity to remind yourself to look at life from different angles.

8. Find the amazing in every routine thing you do. Observe the coordination of something as simple as putting on a watch. We are truly lucky.

9. Look for rainbows. Stop when you see them. Be late. Be amazed.

A genius probably wouldn't...

... let his inner child die.

... let work interfere with fun.

Our path forward

~~~~~~~

In Step 9, we shared the importance of balance in our lives.

In Step 10, we'll explore the secrets of leadership within each of us and how to use leadership to uplift those around us.

DEVELOP
LEADERSHIP
SKILLS

Don't be afraid to go out on a limb,
because that's where the fruit is.
~ Bob Ross

We start in life following. We come full circle when we clear the path for those that follow us.

Wonder Woman, Thor, Iron Man, The Avengers, and lots of comic book figures capture us with made-up heroic rescues from evil villains. We all seem to think of leadership only in terms of fast-acting, larger-than-life rescues from raging waters, hurricanes, or villains. But the heroes I want you to think about are everyday people like you.

One of my tenants phoned me today with news, bad news: She has COVID-19.

A mother of two small children, she works hard to pay her rent while trying to succeed as an independent business owner.

"I've had a raging headache, Steve," she confided. "That was the first indicator that led to being tested and diagnosed."

She knows my recent two-year battle with brain cancer left me immunocompromised. "It's simply not safe for you to be around me, Steve."

She shared her personal medical information; she treated me like family. Her simple act of thoughtful kindness was heroic.

So many going through the COVID-19 pandemic are becoming leaders with the actions they take to protect others. They might not receive an award (or be mentioned in a book), but they are doing the work of heroes and leaders.

Leaders step up and face challenges head-on. They confront conflict with strong and decisive action that is mindful of its effect on others. They develop skills to cope with failure. The outcome isn't always positive or expected.

A major crisis—like this novel coronavirus—defines each generation. Answers aren't easy. Leaders don't come out of the womb ready-made to handle risk-versus-reward decisions on the battlefield or in the boardroom.

Nor in our present situation: the uncharted waters of a global pandemic.

For most of us, leadership is not about responding to world crises, leading a generation, being the head of a country, or being CEO of a company. The most common leadership opportunity faces us at a different but equally important level: learning to be good members of society, raising our families, and taking courageous steps to protect others. That's what my tenant did.

When we help our families and communities face challenges head-on and act responsibly, that's great leadership. People notice. Family first is a great place to start.

We shoulder leadership best when we teach our children to plan and prepare for their futures, when we raise them to be self-sufficient, when we model good citizenship, volunteerism, and political activism. Yet, as all of us find out, no matter how precisely we plan and prepare, life imposes tests, alternate paths, and challenges.

COVID-19 threatened every aspect of the way we live. As The Test of Our Times, it set the course for future generations by our response to it. Its disruption destroyed *everyone's* plans, no matter how originally meticulous, well-intentioned, and thorough.

We need to cultivate leadership, develop the skills and tools for solving life's ever-changing puzzle. We must learn to embrace new situations, use great judgment, act appropriately, and be an agent for change.

Former British Prime Minister Harold Wilson said, "He who rejects change is the architect of decay". Ironically, at a grounded level, the change we need after a rough start is stabilization.

To stabilize, we must embrace the changes we need to make in ourselves by developing great habits and accepting responsibility for everything in our lives. Important leadership skills to develop include:

- Keep your word: Say what you mean and mean what you say. Follow through with your actions. Lead by example. Walk the talk.

- Always leave things better than you find them. At each stop along your way, find a way to improve situations. Each time you pick up litter or clear a hiking trail, you better your environment and strengthen your leadership instincts.

- Don't expect what you don't inspect. Leaders must be productive. You can't produce without results. Never assume work or tasks will be completed unless you continually check to be sure they get done.

- Write often to improve your skills and develop your analytical ability. Effective people communicate regularly (both orally and in writing). These are skills that project who you are. Make that impression clear and understandable.

Learn to multitask, to juggle several jobs or issues simultaneously. Successful leaders keep multiple balls in the air without dropping any.

This is most effective by the honed skills of compartmentalization and prioritizing.

All Aboard

I use a method I call the Infinity Loop. First, sketch the infinity symbol (a horizontal figure eight) onto a drawing board. Next place "stops" (your tasks), at "train stations" around the figure eight, much like the train sets of childhood. Envision a continuous, recirculating path.

I plan my days as though I am riding a train. I make continuous stops to deliver energy to each issue needing attention. When I discover I'm not needed in the moment or the problem is dependent on resolution at another stop, I ride to the next stop. I move issues in and out of my path as time and tasks require.

Along the way, I prioritize and frame with continual reassessments, asking what needs to be done now to accomplish the end goals I've set.

I self-monitor by reviewing how my actions were received at each stop. Followers critically watch every step leaders make. It is good practice to note the reactions of others in order to hone your verbiage, directions, and responses.

Deep down, you know this is true. I'm sure you've watched managers falter, and after seeing those failures, you reflected on how ineffective their leadership was. To achieve the best results, good managers step carefully and deliberately, always trying to do the right thing.

Know the Answers

Powerful leaders willingly undertake the task of shaping lives with counsel and advice. To achieve that, we first need to understand, with depth and conviction, who we are ourselves.

This point was driven home to me several years back at an old cathedral in Cambridge, Massachusetts, where a highly regarded Zen Buddhist monk led a ceremony. I found a seat toward the rear and settled down into a straight-backed oak pew.

The scent of strong incense permeated the room as I waited, one of a hundred sitting patiently for over thirty minutes. At last, the towering doors behind me creaked open and a pristine procession of monks in white robes filed in, smoke wafting eerily from a gold-plated urn at the end of a gold chain, which the lead monk swung gently back and forth.

A short monk, wearing an ornate white pyramid hat and carrying a large staff, trailed in last, ascended to the altar, and stood on a stool behind the lectern. He began chanting and was joined by the others in several, minute-long, guttural "ohmmms."

When the chanting ended, the Zen master accepted questions from the audience.

"Your Holiness," one woman spoke up, "last year I lost my job, and I've been very depressed. Do you think I should spend more time reading Zen teachings or spend more time trying to find a job?"

After a pause, the Zen master stamped his staff hard on the ground and abruptly shouted in a harsh voice, "Who are you?"

Startled, nearly every attendee jumped. Nervously, I strained left and right to gauge reactions, waiting for the other shoe to drop. Instead, nothing happened at all.

The master waited calmly for the woman to respond. When she didn't, he called out, "Next."

A brave soul asked, "How does one enlighten a friend?"

The Zen master responded with two more hard strikes of his cane, and in an equally booming voice asked, "Who are you?"

Did the master want people to identify themselves? Give their names? State which religion they practiced? I was puzzled and more than a little daunted, but fascinated that the master answered a question with a question, an interesting frame.

One by one, the questioners persisted, each countered by the thunderous encore, "Who are you?"

I shrank back into the pew, scared to move, reluctant to ask a question, any question.

Yet another audience member, unabashed, said, "My child has a learning disability, what should I do?"

Although softer in tone, the response was the same. "Who are you?"

When no response came, the Zen master stepped down from the lectern, tapped his staff hard on the altar three times, and proceeded out the back of the church. Obviously, whatever answers were to be given had already been given.

Confused, I didn't know what to make of this harsh display. Several days later, a different interpretation (frame) came to me: We witnessed a masterful performance of exactly what a leader needs to do. This entrancing Zen master led us to understand that the answers to our questions come from within and can only be determined by knowing ourselves.

> ***If you know who you are, you can***
> ***answer your own questions.***

The Zen master was preparing us for leadership, teaching the vital skill of *knowing what to do when there is no one there to tell you what to do.*

Passing the Mantle

My friend Steven graduated from college and went straight to work in his family's business—armed with all the answers of a newly-minted graduate. Four years later, his dad decided to retire early.

A youthful twenty-six, Steven was thrust abruptly into a managerial role. Shortly thereafter, he and his sister bought the company with a loan from their dad. Within days of the transition, Steven came upon a particularly difficult situation and, uncertain, phoned his father.

"Hey, Dad, what should I do?"

"Son, I don't know." His father hung up the phone.

To this day, Steven calls this "the feeling of all feelings"—at a total loss of knowing what to do.

Had his dad practiced tough love or great leadership?

Steven needed to become a leader. His dad knew he had to get out of the way so that his son could grow into the position and shoulder the mantle of responsibility it demanded.

We have all, at some point in our lives, felt what Steven felt in that moment. But he plowed through, kept his head up, and stabilized the business. He figured out what to do, and you can, too.

Leadership is about thinking clearly (as we learned in Step 1) and about rebelling by breaking the outdated practices of the old regime and forging new practices and change. A leader is keeper of the past, holder of the present, and igniter of the future. A leader must also be ready to get out of the way as a new generation ascends. Steven's dad did a great job of igniting Steven's future.

The Importance of Framing in Leadership

There are many philosophies about leadership, each with its own take on self-conduct. One importantly asks us to question authority, suggesting that *leadership is learning and knowing how and when to break the rules.*

Another dates to the ancient Greek philosopher, Aristotle: *Leadership is doing the right thing at the right time for the greater good of one and all.*

What these definitions have in common is that they require leaders to assess situations, make judgments, and act with strength and conviction. To have excellent situation assessment as a basis for action, your frames must be accurate. You must put what is happening in perspective and authorize your followers/workers to accept that frame as actionable truth.

When we understand and assess the situations we confront, we can choose the correct frame to convey our vision. Only then can we choose an action and lead— communicating our vision to those who follow us.

Warren Bennis, the great leadership author, suggests that leaders set the meaning for the organization and, above all, must be persons of trust. He also sees them as figures their followers look to for hope, especially in times of tragedy or great difficulty. Leaders must provide a message of optimism in the face of any circumstance.

Carefully and deliberately using frames to create meaning and offer hope is important work. In his inaugural speech in 1933, Franklin D. Roosevelt famously insisted, "The only thing we have to fear is fear itself." What a great frame to help individuals handle doubt and fear as their country pulled out of the Great Depression.

Additionally, Bennis suggests leaders be predisposed to action, keeping in mind that inaction is also a decision.

President Ronald Reagan, never one for inaction, helped force the removal of the Berlin Wall in 1987 by insisting, "Mr. Gorbachev, tear down this wall!"

Reagan advised leaders that "to sit back hoping that someday, some way, someone will make things right is to go on feeding the crocodile, hoping he will eat you last—but eat you he will."

You cannot hope to guide yourself or others without a basic concept of honor: the acknowledgment of your place and others' places in the world. It is action with respect, seeing others as equals regardless of their station in life. When we gain enough compassion to see those in trouble as friends who've lost their way and need help—rather than as a cumbersome burden, then we are on the path to true leadership.

Seven Tenets of Leadership

As I made my way by managing my business enterprises and guiding my family, I thoughtfully established dimensions to the responsibility of leading others.

1. Teamwork

About five years into my roofing business, a neighbor called the police. When they arrived, he pointed to a ladder on the ground at the site and claimed the initials on it proved my crew had stolen it from him.

We never stole anything. I knew I had paid for and owned that ladder. (If you remember, it was one of my early life lessons to never steal.) Yet right there was the evidence: my neighbor's initials in bold, black marker.

I was befuddled and unnerved. I didn't know what to say.

Things looked pretty bad. Fortunately Joe, one of my employees, had learned to question authority. He walked over to the ladder and rubbed the initials with his fingers. The name came off immediately. Joe turned to the officer and asked him to check the neighbor's pockets. Sure enough, he found a black magic marker.

My neighbor had a lot of explaining and apologizing to do.

Things aren't always as they appear. Question what you think is amiss.

I learned to believe in my team. No one of us is as strong as all of us together. I learned to delegate and unleash the skills of my team-mates, my business partners, my family, and my friends.

I also learned to fully respect others yet maintain a cautious respect for authority ... or the things that pose as authority.

2. Heart

Easy decisions don't often fall onto a leader's plate. Usually the easy decisions are made and handled before those issues get to a leader. More often leaders must make decisions that could potentially harm those on both sides of the problem. There are no easy answers for these dilemmas.

Sometimes, direction must come from the heart—guided by wisdom, knowledge, and understanding of the ripple effects of the decision to be made. That's when an internal compass of fairness and compassion is vital.

Nobody cares how much you know until they know how much you care.

3. Integrity

What are your core values? Do some serious self-examination to know what you truly believe. Integrity represents your conscious choice to adhere to those beliefs and to act in accordance with them. Integrity requires:

- consistent respect for the interests of others.

- willingness to question yourself and your motives.

- principled behavior.

- willpower and honesty to confront poor decisions, yours and others.

- discipline to hold yourself to publicly-productive standards.

Integrity tests your personal ethics and asks you to see beyond yourself, to widen your focus of stakeholders. You must test your actions with a consistency akin to Immanuel Kant's categorical imperative. An eighteenth century philosopher, Kant maintained that motivations for your actions must be consistent and universal.

Building integrity, an exhausting proposition, is worthwhile and rewarding. It develops a personal code of honor that draws on a consistent exploration of difficult-to-honor morals. Resulting decisions honor and reflect not only those stakeholders who are in front of us, but also stakeholders from the past and into the future.

Obviously this kind of integrity is difficult to achieve. But leaders can and should act in ways by which all stakeholders (past, present, and future) could be proud of their actions.

4. Situation Assessment

Before taking action on any issues that arise (within the workplace or the home), give yourself a window of time to consider what might not be obvious at first. Pause. Think it through. And wisely ask questions like:

- Who does the situation affect?

- Are the facts verified?

- What is the quality of the information you are receiving and using?

- How recent and relevant is the information?

- Do you have enough information to make a fair and just assessment?

- What are the global aspects of the situation (outside of those directly impacted)?

- What is the appropriate timing for your response?

After receiving answers, you'll be better equipped to act—as opposed to merely reacting. You may not have the perfect response, but if you have done your work by researching quality questions, you will act with good intent. You will outwork any problems you create and can communicate in a positive manner.

5. Attitude

Leadership is a problem-solving task. To be successful you need a positive, can-do attitude backed with a willing and avid curiosity to unearth the deep roots and connections of issues.

You need an attitude similar to that of fictional private detective Sherlock Holmes: "Come Watson, the game is afoot."

Embrace the contest of wits. Inject positivity, excitement, and satisfaction in solving problems and correcting mistakes.

As you do, you'll find joy in the process.

A word of caution: Never be 100% sure of your responses; employ the 99% Rule to create options and leave 1% wiggle room. Don't be cocky. Allow room for doubt. We all make mistakes. Often what you *miss* controls the outcome, not what you *believe* you know.

6. Myth

Myths are an elusive subject to corral and explain. But leaders need to understand them and the frames they create. Myths control actions, often without our notice or knowledge.

One great example was the myth of Aryan superiority during World War II. Hitler used that fabricated belief to convince his people that Jews were inferior—which sanctioned the Holocaust—with devastating results.

As our perceptions feed into myths, they can become more powerful than reality. Albert Einstein asserted, "Imagination is more powerful than knowledge." In myths, we see that power. Beliefs formed from those perceptions often overtake reason. Hence the phrase: *Beliefs are more powerful than reason.*

Combining these factors, we can see why leaders need to understand how myths are created and how they can be used to impress, to sway, to convince. A successful leader knows when to block potentially harmful, misused myths and when to harness their power for good— much like a super hero.

If we think back to our framing examples in Step 1, which resulted in the Trump presidency, we easily can see why and how myths hold such weight.

7. Initiative

Ready, eager, and willing.

It behooves a leader to be enterprising. That kind of initiative is evidenced by an ability to assess and act, and often to challenge the status quo. Sometimes the direction isn't the most effective or appropriate choice, but it is still an attempt at leadership.

In my classes, whenever a student challenges me, my scheduling, or the materials being covered, I award them a verbal reward: a Leadership Strike for exhibiting leadership qualities (even if sometimes their intentions are questionable).

For instance, in my daylong day intensives, I'm commonly asked, "Can we get out early?"

I respond, "A Leadership Strike for Ms. X. She is attempting to change the outcome. Good for you, Ms. X!"

But I like to put the strike in context. "If I may ask, the last time you bought a gallon of milk, did you buy it in the hopes that the container would be half-full? And if it was, would you return it for your money back?"

The student usually grumbles in a barely audible way as I continue.

"So why would you want to get only half of today's class? It, too, is bought and paid for."

Most often the whole class groans in acceptance of this better frame.

We move on to the materials. The person who attempted to change the outcome felt honored and satisfied with the label (frame) of a

Leadership Strike. Importantly, the students more easily accepted the time they would invest (pay) for a rewarding outcome.

Each time we question rules, challenge the status quo, or attempt to change an outcome, we hone our sense of appropriate action. Just as importantly, the authority figure gets an opportunity to re-assess his or her role. When based on a shared concern, how much better to explore and honor the question and the questioner than to sweep the issue under the rug.

Leaders must determine which fires to light, which to quench, and which to fight and—like great cooks—to monitor the heat for successful results.

Initiative typically has a getting-started phase, when individuals imagine roadblocks and detours in elaborate back-and-forth scenarios. "If I do this, then this will happen, but then I can't do that, so I'll have to do this."

This can create self-sabotage. Instead, plan and envision the job and its outcome. List advantages and disadvantages, but don't delay the project by over-thinking or over-engineering before beginning. Start and re-tool as the job goes along.

My friend Bruce, who has started numerous successful businesses, suggests that projects more easily begin with a Ready-Shoot-Aim approach than they do with Ready-Aim-Shoot.

For example, if you need to dig a hole to install a mailbox, you could analyze the soil, try out several different shovels, research the best shovel for that type of soil, research the perfect-sized mailbox hole, decide on the optimal number of shovel strokes that would be most effective, ... or you could jump to the place you need the mailbox, and start digging with the shovel at hand. The second choice will help you succeed nine times out of ten.

Perfection is the enemy of production.

Forget perfect planning. Jump in and get started to get where you need to go. Course correct as you go. Quick-start habits and continual situation assessment—along with willingness to redirect or adjust—are skills that show initiative.

 **SUMMARY**

Leaders maintain great habits. Their powerful traits include seven dimensions: Teamwork, Heart, Integrity, Situation Assessment, Attitude, Myth, and Initiative. When we take initiative, we don't know whether our action will be a perfect choice, but we know we must act. Using anabolic energy as a guide gives us confidence to act.

Action Steps to Become a Leader

1. Make having a great attitude important.

2. Break the rules in the right way, at the right time, for the right reasons.

3. Reward rule breakers.

4. Jump right into tasks or goals. Don't over-analyze and procrastinate the process.

5. Take care of you! You can't help anyone unless you nurture yourself first.

6. Keep your word and follow through. Leaders must walk the talk.

7. Create a great team and listen to them.

8. Honor everyone's story.

9. Create a mental reservoir. Life plays hardball at unexpected times.

10. Take time away from work. Relax and vacation when possible.

11. Develop your own wisdom.

12. Stabilize, compartmentalize, prioritize, and initiate.

13. Use the 99% Rule.

14. Self monitor.

15. Use the infinity loop to get things done one step at a time.

A genius probably wouldn't...

... *expect others to lead in a group situation.*

→ *Genius thinking: People are natural followers.*

... *wait to be told what to do.*

→ *Genius thinking: Figure out what to do, and do it!*

... *blame others for any shortcomings.*

... *wait to get started on goals, tasks, or projects.*

→ *Genius thinking: Jump right in with both feet and correct your course as you go.*

Our path forward

~~~~~~~~~

In Step 10, we learned how to Develop Leadership Skills, an ongoing exercise we must practice relentlessly. The reward is a better outcome for everyone.

In the Afterword, my dear friend Leobie will introduce our most precious asset.

AFTERWORD

The Ending Is Your Beginning
I fear that with each unnecessary word I speak,
I murder another invaluable moment of your time.
~José Ortega y Gassett

On April 3, 2006, my good friend Leobie entered my office. "Do you have some time, Steve? I'd like to talk."

I knew instantly something was terribly wrong. Of course, I wanted to listen.

Leobie, a vibrant 59-year-old with a heart of gold, had come from the VA Hospital in West Roxbury, Massachusetts, after a doctor had the unenviable task of giving him his prognosis.

Leobie's Story

"There I was, lying in the bed when she walked in and pulled the curtain closed for privacy. I saw concern etched on her face."

She looked me directly in the eye. "I have bad news."

I immediately got a bit sarcastic and thought, *Okaaaaay. So let me ask you for the good news, too. I mean there's always a balance, good news with bad news, isn't there?*

I didn't say anything. I saw how she steeled herself and took a long breath, so I knew this was difficult for her. Even though she hadn't known me before my illness, she rapidly came to know me—in a piercing, slice-to-the-middle way. She even started calling me Lee. Only my friends do that.

I felt strangely detached, as if I were an observer. I usually joke with people at times like this, but I realized this was no time for jokes. I saw the pain in her face. I didn't stop her.

I could sense her inner beauty. Not the kind of surface beauty we all look for at first, but the kind that allowed her to feel and emanate a … a deep empathy.

When she looked at me, she soaked right into me.

"We've found cancer, Lee, cancer in your blood."

Cancer? In my blood? That was the last thing I expected.

Admittedly, I'd entered the hospital feeling drained. The simplest things, like walking to my third floor apartment, left me winded. As it turned out, the doctor had discovered my lungs were full of infection and my kidneys had shut down. I expected pneumonia or something like that. Anything less deadly than stage-four cancer.

A hundred thousand guesses wouldn't have brought cancer to mind. Not even a hundred-thousand-and-one.

It hit me. *I now know what I'm going to die from.*

I mean, maybe I didn't know when. But, yes, I sure knew what was going to do me in.

I cried as I heard Leobie's story. I couldn't handle this devastatingly quick turn in his life.

In the months ahead, Lee did less and less of what we all do—the dumb stuff. He worried less about the hour-to-hour problems of earning his daily bread. Instead, he saw sunshine where there was rain. His legacy was to unite with his children and pass peacefully to a better place.

He did that—and left us sadder for losing him yet hopeful that his charming chorus of encouragement to all of us was his salvation. I miss my true and honorable friend.

His gift to me that day, as he sat calmly telling me his story, was pure wisdom: *Time is all you have. Don't waste it.* I learned a lot from Lee during our time together, but those eight words I will treasure forever.

Heeding Lee's advice, please use *your* time wisely. Share the 10 Steps of *Break the Curse* in the service of others. Remember, *time is all you have.*

To that end, each morning remember to ask, "What is the most effective use of my time today?"

As you break *your* curse by the use of better frames, effective goals, and great mentors, keep those less fortunate than you in mind. They may not have the same skills when faced with temptations and conflict.

Understand and appreciate others with generosity. Build *karma* to help everyone break through to a better life.

May you be as inspired as I by Jean-Jacques Rousseau's famous quote:

What wisdom is there in the world that is greater than kindness?

Thank you for focusing *your* precious time on your legacy of kindness, greater understanding, and building your best life.

Now, go out there and **break *all* the curses**!

STEVE'S 2018 GOALS LIST

1. Each day, ask and answer, "What is the most effective use of my time today?"

2. Lose 25 pounds. Work out on elliptical, swim/ride every other day, yoga.

3. Review my goals daily. Update asset sheet daily. Ask "What am I missing?"

4. Write 200 words a day: *Breaking the Curse* and Elle's book.

5. Access 600k capital from real estate equity for core real estate acquisition growth.

6. Help Dave and Rory build their house.

7. Improve relationship with my beautiful wife and nurture her.

8. Monthly Stinky brats nights with all 4 grandchildren and wife.

9. Do a great job on extending thank yous.

10. Help my family do goals: Be the rising tide that lifts all boats.

11. Hansen Property store remodel, and either sell the back land or start rear site work (1 building).

12. If possible, purchase one significant building for KC.

continued next page...

13. Develop Phil, Dave, Donnie, Niki.

14. Continue teaching at Cambridge College and interviews at Stoughton Media Access Cable.

15. New electric car for Susan. Register 944. Renew 1 truck.

16. Get hoisting license.

17. Identify and Nurture key players: Phil, Dave, Alan, Vin, Sam, Dan, Mark, Gary, Ken, Martie, Kathy, Karen, David ....

18. Do Jersey Devil Triathlon with Stuart.

19. Phil's garage: Keep on working on this.

20. Invest in a 3rd investment property/house in Florida.

21. Identify key business tasks: Leadership, Risk Assessment, Management and Leadership Training, Capital Allocation, Acquisitions, Project Management and Design, Conflict Management, Workplace Execution.

22. Encourage piano for Susan and Elle.

23. Christmas party KC.

24. Be supportive of friends: Luis, Shawn, Stuart, Steve R, Brad, James, Aldo.

25. Vacation 4 times this year. (St. Maarten & Florida)

26. Find round holes for people; square pegs belong somewhere else.

27. Put Dave and Michelle on track for eventual acquisition.

28. Make commitment and preparations to co-sponsor Stoughton's Martin Luther King Day 2019.

BEGINNING YOUR GOALS

Write one goal for each category:

Example # 1: (Physical Health – Lose weight and reduce blood pressure)

Example # 2: (Family – Eat more healthy meals: Cook dinner for family twice per week)

Example # 3: (Work/Career – Create options for upward movement and management)

Category

Timeline
Example (June 2021)

1. Spiritual

_____

2. Emotional

_____

Category

Timeline
Example (June 2021)

3. Financial

_____

4. Physical

_____

5. Family

_____

6. Recreation

_____

7. Work/Career

_____

8. Education/Self-Improvement

_____

Notes about your goals:

_____

_____

_____

_____

_____

_____

_____

_____

_____

_____

_____

_____

_____

_____

_____

_____

STEPPING STONE GOALS

Write one smaller goal for each category to get you started:

Example # 1: (Physical Health – Diet to lose 2 lbs./week - Walk 1 mile every other day)

Example # 2: (Family – Take cooking course focused on healthy eating)

Example # 3: (Work/Career – Take a writing, computer, or tradesman course)

Category   Timeline
Within 90 days

1. Spiritual

_____

2. Emotional

_____

Category	Timeline
	Example (June 2021)

3. Financial

_____

4. Physical

_____

5. Family

_____

6. Recreation

_____

7. Work/Career

_____

8. Education/Self-Improvement

_____

Notes about your goals:

_____

_____

_____

_____

_____

_____

_____

_____

_____

_____

_____

_____

_____

_____

_____

_____

_____

ABOUT THE AUTHOR

Steve Kelley is a graduate of Cambridge College and holds a Master's degree in Management. He is a successful entrepreneur, a real estate developer, a Cambridge College professor of Entrepreneurship, Conflict Management, and Negotiation, a public speaker, a personal coach and mentor, and an author. *Break the Curse: A Template for Change* is Steve's second book. His first book *The Fox Who Sneezed* was co-authored with his granddaughter Elle.

Steve is an active member of his community and enjoys myriad hobbies—training for triathlons, mountain biking, breakdancing, summer ice fishing, and volunteering to help others.

He overcame a rare brain cancer in 2018 and has emerged stronger and more resolved to share his philosophy of reframing our perspectives and positivity with the world.

Steve lives life to the fullest and brings encouragement and joy to all who have the pleasure of knowing him.

He resides in the Boston area in a multigenerational home with his wife Susan, two adult sons, and his beloved grandchildren.

A NOTE FROM THE AUTHOR

To My Dearest Readers,

Thank you for sharing your most precious time with me. As you work on breaking your own curses, believe in yourself.

Life is a race you can win—doing whatever small piece that you can, each and every day!

May the spirit of love and the light of a thousand stars carry you to your dreams.

Warmly,

Steve

— We hope you enjoyed —

BREAK

THE

CURSE

A TEMPLATE FOR CHANGE

10 Steps to Restart Your Life

S TEVE K ELLEY

For more from Steve:
www.BreakTheCurseBook.com

For more from Freedom Press:
www.FreedomPress.org

For more from
One Stop Publishing:
www.OneStopPublishing.com